How to Win and Keep
Your Employees' Hearts

ACE

ACCEPT CHALLENGE ENCOURAGE

OF HEARTS

A
♥

♠

A
♥

BRADLEY SHRADER

Foreword by Michael Woolstrum, CEO Touch International

Publication date: January 2020

ISBN Print: 978-1-7325700-2-3
ISBN eBook: 978-1-7325700-3-0

Library of Congress Control Number: 2019000000

1. Leadership 2. Supervisors 3. Employees 4. Turnover 5. Longevity
6. Onboarding
I Shrader, Bradley. II Ace of Hearts

Ace of Hearts may be purchased at special quantity discounts for sales
promotions, fundraising, or educational purposes for businesses,
schools, and universities. For right and licensing agreements, special
branded printing or to have Brad speak at your event contact him:
aohbook.com

Cover Layout and Design: Megan Van Vuren
Interior Layout and Design: Megan Van Vuren
Editor: Mel Cohen mel@inspiredauthorspress.com
Proofreader: Daniel Kaake
Publishing Consultant: Mel Cohen of Inspired Authors Press LLC
inspiredauthorspress.com
Publisher: Training Lion Press
Printed in the United States of America

*This work depicts actual events in the life of the author as truthfully as recollection
permits and/or can be verified by research. Occasionally, dialogue consistent with
the character or nature of the person speaking has been supplemented. All persons
within are actual individuals; there are no composite characters. The real names
of some individuals have not been used to respect their privacy.*

TABLE OF CONTENTS

DEDICATION

I would like to dedicate this book to my wife, Punnawit. She is an *Ace of Hearts* wife, who loves me and accepts me unconditionally. She makes me feel unstoppable, confident, and capable of doing anything I set my mind to. If every man had a wife just like her, the world would be overflowing with success stories!

Punnawit, thank you for believing in me and always encouraging me to love and accept others unconditionally.

ACKNOWLEDGMENTS

It would be impossible for me to thank everyone in my life's journey who made this book possible.

First, I would like to thank Michael Woolstrum, CEO of Touch International, for not only encouraging me to write this book, but for also taking time out of his busy schedule to mentor me in so many ways. If we had not met, I do not believe I would have ever gotten my spiritual, personal, and professional voice back—completely restoring me to the *Ace of Hearts* leader I once was.

I'd also like to thank my very first *Ace of Hearts* mentor, my seventh-grade science teacher Edmund Crab. He'll probably never know just how much he made me, a shy student that didn't feel accepted by teachers and students alike, feel completely accepted and loved.

Most of all, I would like to thank my God for never giving up on me and showing me immeasurable grace throughout my years.

Hundreds of other friends, family members, and mentors have influenced me in so many ways that have contributed to the writing of this book. I thank all of you.

ACE OF HEARTS

———

ABOUT THE AUTHOR

Brad Shrader has spent most of his life as a serial entrepreneur, launching and owning multiple businesses. He is a successful real estate investor, who has also owned a restaurant, a property management company, and many other successful companies. Brad has also been a chief operating officer of a publicly traded company and a member of the board of directors of that same company.

In 2007, Brad launched his first business website and it grew rapidly. Through that website, he began doing consulting work with companies in that industry. The common denominators he found among most struggling companies were a negative company culture, a lack of effective training, unhappy employees, and a high turnover rate. He noted that rather than there being a cohesive team, there was an us-versus-them mentality between employees and management that resulted in stunted productivity.

Brad looked at his previous experience with online training and realized that although he had been able to help countless companies through high quality training courses, the company cultures of most of his clients still suffered. He began to reevaluate the training he supplied and how it was deployed. Brad discovered that although the content was rich in corporate education, it did nothing to change the company environment.

Brad then began to examine the companies he currently owned, as well as the companies he used to own. He noticed that every company he owned or had once owned had an almost nonexistent employee turnover rate and loyal, productive, happy employees. He spent months interviewing his past and present employees, as well as employees from multiple industries and global CEO's and managers that had amazing company cultures.

Brad gathered all the data he had compiled and found that the common denominator of each great company was that the CEO's, owners, and managers were all *Ace of Hearts'* leaders. Brad also realized that he had always worked to be this kind of leader at his companies.

Brad is committed to helping companies change their culture through training, from top to bottom, in new, exciting, and effective ways via his books, seminars, and the *Ace of Hearts'* leadership courses offered by his company, Training Lion LLC.

FOREWORD

The typical person reads 250 words per minute. Knowing you're taking the time to pick up this book, you're likely above average and will finish the approximately 38,000 words in this book in less than three hours. The average person types 30 words per minute so Bradley physically could have finished typing this book in less than 20 hours. The hours of research and gathering information numbered into the hundreds of hours and were a result of a lifetime of wisdom and sage advice that is being passed on to the reader.

If you'll slow down after each chapter to reflect and contemplate on the time, tested, and true wisdom embedded in the *Ace of Hearts* concept, it will change the trajectory of your life. It did me!

Born into a dysfunctional broken home, I spent my early life in foster care and a boy's home called Century Youth Ranch. Richard and Carol Woolstrum were *Ace of Hearts* leaders by accepting me as broken as I was, challenged me in my relationship with God and people (especially people who had harmed me), and ultimately encouraged and nurtured me with unconditional love. The *Ace of Hearts* Leadership foundation has allowed me to heal from my past while growing in influence as a CEO of a multinational global technology company and bi-vocational pastor of a great church and charitable ministry. I credit this success to God and *Ace of Heart* leaders that have crossed my path challenging me to be better than I could ever have been alone.

———

From experience, I know if you will embrace the *ACE of Hearts* concept Bradley so carefully lays out in this book your life will never be the same. When you do, I would love to read your story. Email me, Michael@woolstrum.com or download Apple or Android play store, BBCPF and connect with me there.

Michael Woolstrum, CEO Touch International

———

WHAT IF...?

W HAT IF YOU were the CEO, manager, or owner of a small business where your employees sincerely looked forward to coming to work? Would you be pleased to know that your employees looked forward to their alarm clocks ringing in the morning? What if they all arose from the bed, excited to shower, get dressed, and fight the traffic—happy to come to work? How would your business run if this were the case? Better and more profitably? Do you think it would make the management of your company easier? Maybe even effortless?

As you finished reading the above paragraph, were you wondering if it's even possible? Did you laugh to yourself and say, "Yeah, right?" Or did you envision how awesome a company you could have if it were possible? It does sound like a fantasy, doesn't it? Why would you think it could never be a reality for your company? All of us could come up with lots of reasons why it would never work.

No One Loves Their Job!

The majority of employees hate going to work! According to a Forbes article citing a recent Gallup poll, 70% of people in the United States hate their jobs. The poll describes 62% of workers as not being engaged at their jobs and putting little energy into their work. Worse news is that 23% hate their jobs to such an extent that they act out and undermine what their coworkers accomplish.

If this is representative of your company, it means nearly two-thirds of your employees are putting very little effort into getting their work done. It also means almost a quarter of your workforce is actively sabotaging the work of the 30% of your workers who don't hate their jobs and are achieving. Are you wondering who fits into what category at your business? Are you also wondering how much profit you are losing thanks to the two-thirds of dead weight and the corporate terrorists who make up another one-fourth? These statistics should get you thinking about changing your company's culture to one where employees love their jobs. These thoughts should also prompt you to plan how you are going to root out and trade off some saboteurs!

What Motivates Workers to Wake Up and Go to Work?

No one is motivated to get up at 5 a.m.—before the sun even pops up—and go to work because they love their job. According to a 2015 Huffington Post article, lack of motivation is the reason Americans down 400 million cups of coffee per day (146 billion cups of coffee per year)! Would you be surprised to learn that 65% of all coffee is consumed in the morning? The old black stuff is going down the hatch for one reason: caffeine motivates. And it motivates many people to go to jobs they hate!

No one drinks coffee for motivation to go out on a date on a Friday night with someone they love. People are not drinking a pot of coffee to find inspiration to go to Disney World. People drink coffee, and lots of it, to obtain the boost they need so they can go punch the time clock. Time clocks only seem to show up at jobs they hate, where they work for a boss they hate even more. I know some people who just love coffee. I am one of them, but I don't need multiple cups to make it through the day. I can drink one cup, or one pot, of coffee, and I enjoy most everything I do. Some people need coffee to survive the day-to-day 9-to-5. We can't make their morning routine more enjoyable, so how can we help? How do we get employees to love their jobs? To not just have to come to work, but want to come to work? And on top of it all, be excited to do so!

Often the first step we need to take is to make the workplace fun and exciting. Management can work really hard to turn the workplace into a better environment. They can sponsor casual dress days, half-day Fridays, and an employee-of-the-month parking spot. They can let employees decorate their cubicles to match their personalities, purchase air hockey tables for the breakroom, and play Twister for an hour before meetings. Oh, I forgot plants. Let them have real plants on their desks! All of those cool things are what make employees happy, right? Problem fixed. Let's move on. Not quite!

It's Not the Main Thing

"Why won't the above suggestions work?" you might be asking. Can't those sorts of office policies change the old company culture we all hate? Aren't change and other related words the popular corporate buzzwords of today? We hear it at every seminar we attend and see it in every management book we read—change, change management, facilitating change, change leadership, company culture change, and more, none of which are bad. In fact, those types of programs are great, but changing company culture is much more.

People hate their jobs for lots of reasons, and the feng shui you incorporate into your office isn't at the top of the list for promoting employee happiness. A pleasantly decorated office is of course a plus, and your brick and mortar workplace should be especially pleasing to your staff. The building, its decor, the desks, the office equipment, and the breakroom are not the "company." The managers, the employees, the vendors, and your customers are the company. All of them combined make up the company and its culture.

COSTCO

Let's look at Costco as an example. I love shopping at Costco each week. I have been shopping there for most of my adult life. Are the products great? Yes, but they're not the only reason I shop there. The décor at Costco is not terrible, but it is not anything special either. There are lots of shelves, lots of bulk items, and a basic floor. So why do I like Costco? Is it the liberal return policy they offer? It's wonderful, but that's not what seals the deal for me either.

Nearly every Costco staff member I have ever interacted with conveys a message of being happy to work there. The vibe of the atmosphere is very upbeat and enjoyable. From the time I am greeted at the front door, usually by name, and throughout my time shopping, the experience is wonderful. Going to Costco is almost like going to church, seeing a dear old friend, or going to a family reunion because many of the employees at my local store know us by name, ask about our family, and always make us feel special. They are more than just some workers. In some strange way, they "do life" with us on shopping day. Remember those two words: do life. You will see them again!

Not only can you feel the difference in the employees, but there is also something different about the customers who shop at Costco. Costco has a company culture rich in giving the customer a pleasant and positive shopping experience. That experience wears off on Costco customers and, in my mind, molds them into the Costco company culture. Imagine if the Costco culture could not only infect the customer with pleasantness, but also wear off on the communities around Costco. There would be some real contenders out there for the friendliest city and town competitions we hear about every year!

I sometimes joke that if I were going to get a tattoo, it would be of my Costco membership card on my left forearm so I could show it to the employee checking customers at the front door. I am sold on Costco—a customer for life, as long as their company culture does not take a nosedive!

What Is Important?

We've now determined that it's not just the physical environment at your company that is important. The company is truly made up of its employees. So what are some nuances we need to examine when it comes to the people who work at your company? What are some factors to consider concerning employees and their level of workplace happiness? What is important to them?

EMPLOYEES AND THEIR DIFFERENCES

How about all the personalities, ideas, and differences people have? There's bound to be unhappiness, conflict, and stress when you throw a bunch of people and their idiosyncrasies into a building together for eight or more hours. Their only escape from a coworker they don't gel with may be a 30-minute lunch break or a few minutes hiding in a bathroom stall! There are going to be things people do not like about each other. It may be the way someone looks or something about their personality. Often it will be their political label or their thoughts on current, hot button social issues, or it might be for no reason at all. Their style of work, how they lead a project, or how they perform their duties may irritate other people. Jealousy or anger may be aroused by coworkers who don't do their fair share of the work, forcing their colleagues to have to pick up the slack. Some workers may think someone is working too hard, making them look bad. We can't change people's personalities and we certainly cannot brainwash people into thinking or voting differently, so how can we change employees and their interactions with one another?

I NEED A RAISE, AND AFTER THAT, ANOTHER RAISE

Salary is one thing that is important to every employee. People have bills to pay, and if they are not able to pay their bills, it puts a lot of stress on them. This stress inevitably spills over into the workplace. Employees might physically be at work, but their mind might be thinking about the stack of bills on their kitchen table. They might be stressed out and mentally consumed about being behind on their car payment. It's hard to be productive at work when you are worrying about the repo man towing away your car from the employee parking lot.

A 2018 article in Inc. Magazine states that 70% of workers who responded to their survey were either actively seeking new jobs or thinking about it always, often, or sometimes. We can't always pay more, and sometimes another company pays better. So how do we retain employees who are salary-driven and looking to find employment elsewhere?

I HATE MY BOSS

While doing some employee satisfaction surveys through my company, Training Lion (https://traininglion.com/), I learned that nearly 30% of employees hate their bosses' guts. Exit surveys done on employees leaving companies showed 51% of people quitting their job were doing so because they hated their job.

I was doing some consulting for a company I used to own because the new owner had retention rates lower than a root cellar. When I owned the business, it had been rare for one of my employees to quit, and I think I only fired one employee during the entire time I owned the company. After spending less than a day with the new owner, I immediately discovered why employees were quitting on a weekly basis. He

mistreated them, screamed and cursed at them, and made them feel worthless. He paid extremely well, with some of his employees making nearly six figures a year; however, pay is not much of a motivator. On the other hand, respect, communication, direction, and a few other factors are.

I have been told that every manager is going to be hated, and if they are not, then they aren't doing their job. I totally disagree with this thought process. It's not only wrong, but it leads to dissent, a high staff turnover rate, and low productivity. In effect, it results in much lower profits for companies. How do you find the balance between being a boss who isn't hated and a boss who isn't a pushover?

PROMOTIONS AND POSITIONS

Promotions are a wonderful way to motivate employees and improve workplace morale. The result can be higher productivity in your company and successfully retaining your most talented employees. Promoting from within recognizes and rewards employees who perform and makes them feel valued. The person who receives a promotion will be more motivated and more loyal to management and the company. It sets them up for success in the company, as well as prepares them for more tasks, responsibilities, and future promotions.

Many employees are looking for advancement and titles. When people do not see a chance for promotion, they often become disenchanted and unproductive. This can be a problem because every business has managers, but not everyone can be successful in a managerial position. When the chance for a promotion arises, mayhem can break loose. A lot of employees feel they deserve a certain promotion, a particular title, or the corner office with a view.

In my consulting, I witnessed an organization almost be destroyed over one promotion opportunity with a small $1,500 raise. The position was narrowed down to two equally qualified candidates who would have been great supervisors. The two happened to be best friends personally and professionally. Sadly, their friendship did not survive the promotion process.

Immediately a heated competition broke out between the two candidates' teams, to prove who would be the better leader at producing results. Both candidates began to go to upper management with reasons why they were better than the other, and weeks of backbiting ensued. Management handled the whole process totally wrong. They made promises to both parties they could not keep, pitted them against each other, and used the opportunity to push production to its limits. I believe they enjoyed the war! Some heated arguments between the two candidates occurred, which I feel should have disqualified both. The result was that one candidate quit when he did not get the promotion and the one promoted quit three years later. Both men's teams were disgusted with the whole situation, and morale suffered for several years. Most members of both teams moved on in time. The company's retention rate was at an all-time low due to all parties exiting the company within a few years.

Not everyone can be promoted, and some employees will be promoted over others. This can lead to envy, strained relationships among coworkers, and lots of dissatisfied employees. How do you manage promotions and keep everyone happy?

It is Possible

I have owned multiple companies and employed scores of people who have loved their jobs and looked forward to coming to work every day. When I tell people that, they sometimes laugh and say my employees were lying. Under the right circumstances, that could be true, but I have evidence disproving the theory.

I am a serial entrepreneur and have owned several companies. Often, after I grew a company to profitability, another company or competitor would buy the company. On multiple occasions when this happened, I was able to witness the employees' journey presale and post-sale. I routinely saw fiercely loyal members of my staff become disloyal. Hard-working employees went from productive to unproductive. Employees went from having great attendance to calling off regularly. I saw long-term former employees of mine quit suddenly under the new management for no apparent reason. What I saw the most was a totally different countenance on the faces of those employees, ending up in the downgrading of the company culture under the new management.

Feedback

Over the years, I've received unsolicited feedback from former employees. It's always the same overall message from dozens of employees:

- I loved working for you and have hated every job I've had since then.
- I've never felt as hopeful about work as when I worked for you.
- I always knew you cared about us.
- I loved coming to work every day.
- If you hadn't sold the company, I would have retired under you.
- I've never forgotten those days and I fear I'll never love another job again.
- I always know, after all these years, I can still call you for advice or help if I need it.
- I remember being in your office and you giving me advice on my personal life. I didn't follow it, and I ruined my life. Nearly every day I hear your words in my head and I think, "He cared so much. Why didn't I listen?"
- I always knew you wanted me to be successful not only in my job role, but in my life too.
- You were really interested in me, in my well-being at work and outside of work.
- Thank you. Working for you changed my life completely.
- I cried when you sold the business, and I've missed you as a boss ever since.
- You taught me everything about your business without worrying about my one day becoming your competitor. I've owned my own company for nine years now, and you still take my calls and mentor me.
- While working for you, you taught me about business and even more about successful living.

Did all of my employees leap out of bed every morning, thrilled to come to work for me? It wasn't every day, but call-offs and showing up late were rare occasions. And it wasn't every employee who loved their job, but nearly all of them did. There were ups and downs on the clock and off the clock, but I "did life" with them. There it is again! They knew I never wanted to give up on any of them and I would always be there to help them when they would let me.

Not every single day is going to be perfect, and certainly not every employee is going to perform at 100% all of the time. Life's tragedies happen in people's personal lives and spill into the workplace. Similar ups and downs of life occur inside the company, affecting business operations. This will never change, but it can be mitigated. Sadly, such mitigation is often reactive rather than proactive.

In fact, some employees just don't make it. You can train, teach, guide, and correct some people's behavior and still not get the results you desire. It may be that they don't catch onto the skills you need them to learn. They could be in the wrong role, your training program may be flawed, or they may not be the right fit for your business. In the end, employees who are not working out will leave: either on their own or by your making the decision for them. Whatever the reason, this too needs to be mitigated.

WHAT IS THE RESULT?

Having a company people like working for has lots of benefits. When employees love coming to work, the business runs at an optimal level. The hours spent at work are enjoyable, profits are up, call offs are low or nonexistent, and employee turnover is never an issue. In fact, when your employees love to come to work, word gets out. You'll never be short on great talent seeking you out asking for a job. The biggest reward is knowing that your staff knows you love and value them. They will know you are not only interested in making company profits, but you are interested in them as well. They'll know you take a genuine interest in them as a valued person, not just as an expendable employee.

WHAT NOW?

A successful company culture requires more pieces to the puzzle than redecorating the office and making the workday into a giant pep rally. In the following chapters, we are going to examine what will bring real change to your organization. I'm going to identify certain aspects of the workplace that are important to employee happiness and others that you might think are on top of the important list but are really not. Once I identify the most important and least important factors, you will learn what activates each one and how they will help to bring about real culture change to your organization.

Your Company's Identity

WHAT MAKES UP the identity of your company? What brands your organization? Is it your high-quality company logo? A logo is a pretty big deal. It identifies your brand, and with a great marketing campaign, people will see your logo and immediately identify it with your company's name. The Nike swoosh, adopted in 1971, is one of the most recognized logos in the world today. How recognizable? At least $27 billion recognizable!

Then there is your company's unique selling proposition (USP). It must be an important identifier too, right? A short, descriptive phrase identifies the value your business creates. It differentiates you from your competitors. "Built Ford Tough," "Just Do It," and "Have It Your Way" are all slogans that resonate with most everyone. However, it isn't simply the image or logo you want to portray to the public. As a marketer, you must accurately convey what is unique about your business to be successful in a crowded market of homogeneous competitors. Without pinpointing your uniqueness, you can't successfully target your sales efforts.

One of the companies I used to own serviced the auto finance industry. It had the coolest logo! It was a bulldog's head with a spiked collar and sharp teeth. This company also had a cute USP, "We Take a Bite out of Your Past Due Accounts." My clients identified the USP with my company. My logo and my USP were both an important part of my company's identity.

I used to send out coffee mugs and candy containers with my logo, USP, and phone number proudly displayed. I sent out chocolate candy custom-branded with bulldog wrappers to all of my clients. Every one of my clients' account representatives had one of my company mugs on their desk. In every breakroom, you'd find my candy containers filled with chocolates on the countertop. I regularly sent chocolate to refill the candy containers.

Other times I sent out company polo shirts, ball caps, mouse pads, and a plethora of other customized promotional items to my clients. I wanted them to think of my company, my logo, and my memorable motto all day long. Eventually I controlled the lion's share of my service industry, was the largest in the Midwest, and was used by customers all over the country. Two dozen or so other competitors, if combined, controlled maybe about 10% of the work I wasn't doing.

I thought I had branded my company well, and I worked hard to make sure all of my hard work and marketing paid off. However, I found out that although my branding had helped me get business, it was not the only thing that had clients coming to me in droves. In fact, it was not the main thing.

On a routine sales visit to one of the nation's largest finance companies located in Michigan, I found out what the real reason was. I saw so many of my coffee mugs, candy containers, and chocolates all over the building, I wasn't sure if I was at a branch office of my own company or at my client's office. Truthfully, I saw more of my logos than the logos of the customer I was visiting!

Whenever I visited a customer, I always liked to do some quality assurance regarding my company's performance. I could ask the managers how my company was doing, but this approach never provided accurate feedback. It was the frontline collections representatives who interacted with my company, not the top people.

On this sales visit, I bought individual pizzas and soft drinks for every account representative in the building. I did this for three reasons. One, so I could thank them for giving me their business. Two, so I could brand my company further, and three, so I could interact with the people who interacted with my people. As they grabbed their food and began to eat, I circulated throughout the collections department, stopping by to chat with each of them, introduced myself, and inquired on how we were doing.

While there, I was able to talk with nearly every

representative. I asked them what we could do better, what we should keep doing, and what we should stop doing. I told them to give me honest feedback, whether it was good, bad, or ugly. I was shocked to get a whole lot of good and, even better, some feedback indicating we exceeded expectations.

Reoccurring comments I received from my Q and A covert operation:

- Your employees are always happy to help us.
- They never seem bothered, and it's almost like they love what they do.
- They are willing to go the extra mile for us.
- Your company really has a unique spirit.
- We have gotten to know your employees well because, unlike other companies we deal with, your people stick around.
- They always speak well about working for you and your company.

One employee actually said she enjoyed talking with my staff so much, she sometimes called just to talk because she always felt better after the call. She then asked me to come up and teach her managers how to make her company more positive and enjoyable.

My final conversation was with the collection's manager. She assured me we were doing a great job and that my services and staff always exceeded expectations. She told me that all of her vendors gave them promotional items, but such gifts were never going to earn them any new or additional business. The reason why we were the preferred company was that her team absolutely loved my entire staff. She claimed it was my employees who branded my company. She then leaned towards me and said, "But keep sending us chocolates. We love them too!"

It seems the most important facet a company has may not be the products, the services, the logo, the slogan, or the mission statement. It's your people! The success of your organization lies largely within the employees you have working for you. And, as mentioned in Chapter 1, there are a whole lot of unhappy employees out there.

Your company's identity is their identity. Who your employees are for those eight or more hours a day, five days a week is going to be there for the world to experience. Not only do they represent you during work hours, but they are also a reflection of your company on their off time. Whether they are spending time on social media, going out for dinner, shopping for groceries, or speeding down the road, they carry you and your company with them.

"They are on their own time, so how can that be?" you might be asking yourself. In this day of social media, you do not want employees posting publicly how much they hate working for you. Even worse, you don't want your employees posting something undesirable on behalf of your company. Having your company associated with racist, sexist, or other offensive comments posted by one of your employees is never good for your company's identity.

Imagine you are having coffee while watching the news

before you leave for work in the morning. Suddenly a breaking news story alert comes on about a suspect making online threats to the President on social media. The news anchor announces the person's name, and you realize it's one of your employees. You quickly look on Facebook and find their account. Right there under "Work," you see your company listed. You shriek in horror when you realize that thousands upon thousands of people are looking at your employee's profile and learning they work for you! It won't be a red-letter day for your company. One employee's behavior will brand your company in a way no logo, slogan, or mission statement ever will.

Are you wondering how you can avoid an embarrassment like that? You can't control what your employees are sharing on social media, can you? You cannot, but you can hire the right employees who won't engage in such behavior. You can impact the people you hire with positive hiring, onboarding, and training processes. You can develop a company culture where your employees love coming to work, culture that positively changes how your employees feel about coming to work each day, and a culture that positively impacts your employees' families and friends.

Imagine if such a change didn't stop there but eventually trickled out to make the community around your company a better place to live. What if multiple companies in multiple cities followed suit and created companies whose employees sincerely loved working for them. The corporate world and the real world could be changed in a great way!

What would it do for your company? And your profits? If we can help our employees enjoy coming to work and have better lives, the benefits would be innumerable for your company and the community. When we invest in our employees and help them succeed not only in the workplace, but also in their personal lives, it is a game changer for everyone. When your employees have a better quality of life, those around them in their personal lives will benefit as well.

Investing in your employees makes them better citizens! And better citizens care about their homes and the neighborhoods they live in. They care more about the city they live in and often become involved in community activities. They build lasting and meaningful relationships with their neighbors and fellow citizens. They become community assets through volunteering, philanthropy, and local churches.

When people are happy and content with their jobs, they are less apt to relocate to another city. Staying longer turns them into permanent and positive fixtures in their community. Those folks will invest in the local economy by spending their money at area businesses. They will buy groceries, household goods, cars, and houses.

Happy employees will do most of the working, spending, and living in your company's city. They can not only be your lifelong employees, but also help build a thriving local economy that will produce even more customers for your company. Investing in your employees will be nothing but positive for you and your company's profits.

How does having employees who look forward to coming to work affect your company internally? It is hard to quantify and sometimes hard to recognize the effects. You may never know the full impact it can have. The impact may be revealed when one of your customers expresses to you how much they enjoy working with your employees. On the other hand, never hearing those words from one of your customers doesn't mean it's not happening.

The amount of revenue being recorded is not the only proof that your company culture is paying off. It isn't always about dollars and cents, and it doesn't always mean business is booming. It can also be identified in the little things, such as employee dedication, teamwork, and/or efficiency. Those things are impossible to quantify on a spreadsheet or have your accountant crunch the numbers on. You might try to put a pencil to all of the factors, and you might see some return on your investment with an improved company culture.

Of course, you may never get a full report, or it may come years later. Such a report may not be issued by an auditor or show up on some computer software used to calculate unseen debits and credits. It may come from one of those happy employees, years later when they surprise you with a detailed report you never fathomed existed.

Ten years after I sold one of my companies, I was able to reconnect with one of my former employees. She had been a great employee, and I felt I had treated her well. Here is the report I was given about her time working for my company.

What do I think of Brad Shrader as a boss? To be honest, I think of many things when I think of him. He was someone who really wanted to see me make progress in life and do better for myself. He was a true friend, someone who I knew had my best interest at heart and sincerely cared about me. I felt more like

a family member than an employee. Everyone who worked at the company were all like family. We all looked out for one another and were willing to help each other any way we could. Everybody at the company worked as a team player, and nobody acted like they were better than anyone else. The work environment was absolutely wonderful, and we were all happy to come to work. It was a place I wanted to be a part of.

I know it sounds strange and a bit unreal, but even though we worked very hard, we enjoyed the work. We all worked hard, but not just because we wanted to. We wanted to do it for Brad. It was because he treated each of us as a human being, not just as an employee. He took a sincere interest in each employee. It didn't matter if it was about your home life or a question about work; you knew you could go to him about anything. He would always be there for you, whether he agreed with you or not.

When Brad sold the company, the new owners took over and turned it into a terrible place to work. No one was excited to go to work anymore, and no one wanted to be there anymore. The teamwork vanished, and helping each other out disappeared too. There always seemed to be a lot of tension in the air, and the employees seemed to always conflict with one another.

All the employees knew the new owners didn't care about them, if they were there or not. We all felt like a number instead of a human being. It made everyone feel like they didn't care about the company either.

It wasn't long before I chose to stop working there. I packed up and I moved back to my hometown, knowing in my heart if Brad would have kept the company, I would still be there working for him. He made me feel special, made me feel wanted and valued, and made me feel part of a family. It wasn't just me. He was that way with everyone who worked there. When you have a boss who makes you feel that way, one who shows an interest in you and truly cares, you want to come to work. And it makes you want to work hard for him and do your best. It makes you feel different about work because it doesn't really seem like work.

The only way, at the time, I felt I could pay him back for the way he treated me was for me to be the most productive employee I could be. I truly did my best for him. To this day, we stay in contact every few months through Facebook. I know if I had a problem, or if I needed anything, I could reach out to Brad. Working for him made us lifelong friends, and I know I can go to him for anything in the world. He'd be there for me even if it's just to listen to me talk.

For me and the other employees, he was more than a boss. He was our friend, a true friend, and I loved him like family. He was a true inspiration in my life at a time when I really needed it, because I was in a relationship that was very bad and in a new city.

I really had nobody: no family or friends. But Brad, being the big-hearted person he was, knew what was going on even without me telling him. After work, I'd be at home, and sometimes he would just pop in just to check on us to make sure we were fine or to see if we needed anything. Brad was a very special person and boss. He was fair to everyone, and he was always willing to help anybody in their life. At that time in my life, if I had not started working for him, I don't know where I would have been. But because of him, I knew I deserved better, and he made me want a better life.

   – Alison Whittenburg Swift

The feedback I received from Alison took me by complete surprise. I never knew just how much I had impacted her professional and personal life. I cared about all of my employees, but I didn't know just how it much it had affected them. I never saw any of them as a number, but as individuals. I felt responsible for each employee. I was running a business, not just providing services or products for my customers but also providing for my employees.

I had the huge responsibility of bringing in enough business to pay each employee a living wage, enough business to pay them better than the living wage at the time! They had families to provide for, and I knew if I failed them, I would also be failing their families. I also knew failing their families would be failing our community. I wasn't building my company just for me but for them as well.

I invested in each employee professionally and personally. I felt an employee was not just someone who took up space for eight hours each day. Each of my employees was a person with a life outside of my business—a life filled with highs and lows, hurts and happiness, and a whole lot of in-between! I took an interest in those lives so I could understand my employees better and help them be a success in every area of their life.

I wasn't just a boss at the job, and I didn't want them to just be my employee. I wanted to see them succeed not only on the clock and off the clock, but also in every area of their life. My goal was not to do eight hours a day with them, but to "do life" with them, which is exactly what we did together!

What Do They Have in Common?

WHAT DO A single father, a soldier suffering from post-traumatic stress disorder, a three-time divorcee, a single parent, a Christian, a Muslim, an Orthodox Jew, a woman in an abusive relationship, a progressive Democrat, a conservative Republican, a vegan, a deer hunter, and a functioning alcoholic all have in common?

They make up the potential future workforce of your company! And I could add hundreds of other diverse categories of employees to the list, making the above question a candidate for the Guinness Book of World Records' longest question.

Besides making up today's workforce, they also share other commonalities. Although each employee is somewhat unique, they all are trying to fit in with your company. They want to be accepted by both company management and their colleagues. Day one through their last day on the job can be very stressful, just trying to gel with all of the strangers with whom they spend twenty to forty hours a week. There are bound to be issues among coworkers who spend over 2,000 hours a year together.

Remember being the new kid at your new school? Or your first day in class with a bunch of kids you really did not know? Do you remember going to kindergarten on the first day? You were yanked out of the comfort and safety of your home, separated from your loving parents, and dropped off somewhere brand-new. There were new faces and names to learn, new rules to follow, and on top of that, schoolwork to do.

Of course, when you were a student, you had some breaks away from the classroom known as recess, which were quite daunting too. Small cliques of your classmates gathered together on the playground, picking and choosing who would be accepted and who would not. There were the cool kids, the bullies, the sporty kids, the introverted nerds, and so on. If you did not fit into one group or another, you were on the outside looking in.

Then there were the teachers, administrators, coaches, and other school staff. They had their pet students as well. Those students who were on the favorites list had it easier than those who were not. The potential favors included sports teams, classroom choice, extracurricular activity preferences, and other privileges.

It's much the same in today's corporate world, except the students are older and the teachers are the supervisors, managers, and business owners. Being the new employee at a new place of employment is very hard for most people. The newbie at the company is confronted with a sea of new faces, names to put to those faces, and a new set of rules to follow. Then there is the task of learning to correctly perform the tasks that go along with their new job. Just like school, there are still cliques, bullies, and the stress that comes with trying to fit in and find your place. Will the new employee be accepted by his new coworkers? Will he make it past his probationary period? Will his supervisors like him?

WHAT ELSE DO THEY HAVE IN COMMON?

I have conducted interviews with hordes of employees in all sorts of industries. As I spoke with these employees, I noticed the numerous similarities in what they each said. All of them seemed to have one common feeling. Let's look at some of the interview responses people gave me.

TRUCKING

Bob R. had been in the trucking industry for 17 years. He never liked any of the trucking companies he worked for. Sure, there was always a honeymoon period when he would be hired on with a new company, but it was always short-lived. He felt that at every company, his onboarding and training experience was always negative, incomplete, and disorganized. Dispatchers, drivers, dock workers, and managers didn't really understand the other people's job roles, responsibilities, and challenges. That misunderstanding seemed to lead to a lot of conflict between departments and employees. One suggestion he had to eliminate those misunderstandings was to have employees spend time in each other's roles. If they could have a better grasp on the other employees' roles, they would be more patient with each other.

Management would often implement rules that hindered work progress. They would never explain the reason for the rule and would never ask the frontline employees the repercussions of such rules. He had enjoyed working for his current employer when it had been family owned. The drivers and other employees used to all get along and would help each other out. The company was sold to a larger company, and almost immediately a more "corporate" atmosphere developed. The new manager seemed to rule with an "iron fist" and worked hard to conquer and divide the employees. Bob said that since the new company took over, he has always felt expendable and even remembers his boss addressing him as driver 57. Not calling Bob by his name made him feel less than human.

Hospital

Kate Z. has worked at one of the nation's most renowned hospitals for nearly three decades. She describes her time there as "doable." She complained that hospital management never asked the employees who did the work anything about policy and procedure development. Instead, they would just implement a policy about something they were completely unfamiliar with and hope for the best. Rarely was there a best, and usually the new policy resulted in more work and lots of problems for her and her coworkers. Whenever the children of one particular colleague were ill, management would go out of their way for that employee. They would give that employee time off or let them make more than the allowed number of personal phone calls. If an employee's parent passed away, management would usually put up a note about the funeral arrangements, urge coworkers to attend the funeral, and collect money to buy flowers. But Kate recalled that when her mom died, not one word was said, no flower money was collected, and not one coworker came to the funeral home. Kate is an introvert and was already not feeling accepted at work. She blamed her introverted personality for the lack of response to her mom's death. "I just felt worthless, like I didn't exist in anyone's eyes," she said.

The Railroad

I was able to talk to dozens of employees of one of the largest railroads in North America. Nearly every one of them was making over $100,000 a year, but they all hated their jobs! Their dirty laundry list on what made them miserable was extensive. How they paid back the company for what bothered them was twice as long! They felt used and abused by their supervisors and saw them as the enemy. One man told me that when his wife was due to have a baby, his supervisor told him, "You work for the railroad, and that is your life. Don't ask for time off, and if you call off, I will see to it you're fired. You'll get to see your kid by the time he's in high school. Now go move some trains." Managers would hide in the bushes and place obstructions in switches, with the hopes of catching conductors violating safety rules. They would then walk up and say, "You're fired," and send the man home. Fired seems like an over-the-top word to use in this situation, and what it meant was that he'd be off for a few weeks pending an investigation and hearing. Then the union would have to fight for the employee to get his suspension lessened or get his job back if he had prior violations.

Conductors and engineers were on what's called an "extra board." This meant they did not know what time they were going to go to work or what time they would be off.

They were always on call, with a two-hour show-up time. They had to sleep in hotel rooms, and they were only off for ten hours before they would be called back again. Often, they'd work the 12 hours allowed by the Federal Railroad Administration, then sit in a parked train for several hours, waiting for a cab to pick them up.

These employees showed up for work with the goal of costing the company time and money. They would engage in "slow walking" to delay work. Several employees told me their two favorite statements were "We ain't going to leave this rail yard today" and "We are not going to build one train on this shift." The twelve-plus hours they worked were filled with negativity and complaining about the company. Nearly every employee told me they felt like a robot rather than an employee. They knew if they died today, the supervisors would forget their name before the shift was over, and trains would keep on rolling down the tracks.

FOOD SERVICE

Servers, bussers, and kitchen staff interviews revealed that most restaurant employees feel management treats them as if they have no value. They felt they were talked to in a disrespectful manner, put under a lot of pressure, and paid too little. Many of them expressed a feeling of hopelessness about their job, and they suffered from low morale and depression. Nearly every person I spoke with felt they performed their duties very well, but their diligence was never recognized by supervisors. They felt the reason was that most customers don't communicate positive feedback to managers; only negative feedback is given. One chef at a five-star hotel told me this consistently, though there was a low percentage of complaints about his food. He said people have different tastes, and not everyone is going to like his food. He felt as though his supervising chef often treated him unfairly, focusing on the 2% or less of his customers who complained. The 98% of people who ate his food loved it, but it was never acknowledged. A common statement was that they did not want to be treated like a friend by management, but rather just like a human being. More than one person I spoke with said they felt dehumanized by the way their supervisors treated them.

SECURITY

I spoke with over fifty employees who worked at one of the largest security companies in the world. They all felt overworked, underpaid, and underappreciated. Most of them said their managers would not communicate with them, would talk down to them, and didn't care about them. They were often bounced around from one security site to the next without warning. If their relief did not show up, they found themselves stuck at their post and unable to leave. They would be told that if they abandoned their post, they would be fired. When a relief person failed to show up, management was never in a hurry to find a replacement, and the employee was often forced to work a double shift without notice. Not being able to leave their post, they usually worked another eight hours without any food and sometimes no water.

One security guard told me that a human resources officer called her at home while she was off work from a recent surgery. She said he was very rude and kept demanding to know when she could return to work. He threatened to have her replaced if her return date was not soon. She said she was in a lot of pain and had not been released to go back to work by her physician, but he did not seem to care. She started to cry and shared with me how she had asked him to please keep her job open. While she was on the phone with him, she started to cry, so she let him know she had lost her baby and then undergone a complete hysterectomy. She said he loudly interrupted her and told her he didn't care, that he didn't need to know what kind of surgery she had, and that it was inappropriate for her to tell him. He then hung up on her. As she wept, she said, "Brad, I am a human being. I lost my baby and then went through a major surgery. None of it mattered to him. He acted as if I was a stray dog that didn't deserve any compassion." In talking with security personnel from this company, I heard over and over that they were seen by management as just a security uniform, rather than a person.

LAW ENFORCEMENT

After talking with over a hundred police officers, corrections officers, and 911 dispatchers, I have concluded that the heroes of our streets deserve better. Law enforcement men and women work swing shifts, long hours, weekends, and holidays protecting you and me. Their lives are at risk on a daily basis. They are often assaulted and even spat on. The high level of stress they work under takes a toll on their bodies, their minds, their marriages, and their other relationships. Those who choose careers in law enforcement are rarely dispatched to a scene for anything positive and certainly not to receive any praise for doing a good job. Instead, they are dispatched to scenes of violence, death, and destruction. They perform their duty day after day, often dealing with the dregs of society without complaint. Suicide, depression, post-traumatic stress disorder, alcoholism, and dying in the line of duty (or at an early age) is often the reward they receive for what they have experienced for 40 hours a week for twenty or thirty years of service. More than once I've heard that supervisors don't care about them and treat them poorly. One officer told me he approached his police chief about some mental anguish he was going through as a result of all of the blood, gore, and violence he had witnessed over 25 years of working for the city. His chief brushed him off, saying, "Do you think you are the only copper who has issues? Hit the street, Nancy. I don't have time for you."

From the Mouths of Managers

In talking with various people in management positions, I was able to get the other side of the story. I found it to be most shocking. I encouraged the supervisors and managers I was talking with to speak candidly, which only confirmed what I had been told by their employees.

"I rule with an iron fist!" said an oil and gas manager. "I've got them in golden handcuffs," he exclaimed. "When some nobody lucks out and gets a six-figure job here at the refinery, I can treat them any way I please."

"I don't care what they have to say. I am in charge, and if they don't like it, there's the door!" said one operations manager at a steel company.

"I run this prison like a well-oiled machine. I'll break down a correctional officer before my machine breaks down," the Major of a state prison stated.

A supervisor at a pharmaceutical company told me, "Employees are like children, and they need to be treated like children. I keep a close eye on them, and occasionally I must spank one of them. A good whipping keeps the kids in line."

An executive at a tech firm shared, "Fear motivates, and I utilize it every day. They know if they don't work their butts off, they are outta here."

A manager at an office revealed, "I don't trust one of these (expletive). They will steal everything they can from you, whether it's hours or paperclips."

One school administrator felt all his teachers were lazy and felt entitled. He said, "Brad, if it wasn't for the teacher's union, I'd boot all of them out the back door. There is not one of them I like or respect."

I could list more of the same, as revealed above, from both managers and employees of many other industries. Are you seeing the recurring theme being communicated in each of these industries? Employees are not being treated like human beings but like something much less!

How could anyone treated like this be happy to come to work? It would be impossible to be productive working in the types of work environments described above. There could never be any sort of company loyalty developed by these employees. Employee longevity can't be realized when people work under these sorts of conditions.

Managers often complain to me about their company's

high employee turnover rate and how their best employees are always leaving. That is certainly something to complain about. Not only is it costly, but when good people walk out the door, it is also disruptive to operations. It hurts morale and sometimes will prompt others to seek new employment. These managers like to blame high turnover problems on everything but the real reason. Employees don't leave jobs; they leave horrible managers and supervisors.

They leave managers who overwork them and underappreciate them, supervisors who only see poor performance rather than the positives and the ongoing contributions employees make. Employees flee from supervisors who don't care about them and have no interest in building a relationship with them. No one wants to give eight to ten or more hours a day to a company when management does not care about them. Employees can and will be passionate about their job and the company they work for when their bosses are passionate about taking an interest in their employees.

OPPORTUNITY AND REWARD

CEOS, small business owners, and managers all have an incredible opportunity to be influential guides and mentors to this generation of workers. They must learn how to deal with the different types of people they employ with all of their personality differences. They must be willing to change how it has always been done, to replace the old way of doing things with the new way—something entirely new and different.

Yesterday I had lunch with a thirty-year-old man whom I will call Joe. He is the embodiment of the type of employee you might be considering hiring. He hates big corporations. He thinks all CEOs and shareholders are greedy and overpaid. Joe is certain employees aren't cared about or valued at all in today's corporate world. Money isn't all important to him, but the work environment is. Work relationships and being treated fairly by his employer mean everything to him. He told me if he truly felt valued by a company and treated more like family, he would be willing to work harder, be more productive, and be a more loyal and committed employee. "I could be one of those company men!" he exclaimed.

Joe also expressed that he had a huge desire to be a part of something when it came to where he worked. He was looking for more of a relational community of people than a corporate structure. Joe said emphatically that he wasn't interested in marching into some building, punching a clock, and being a body to fill a cubicle. He expressed a strong desire to be accepted by coworkers and management alike. He stated that he wanted to have a voice and be involved in building something successful. His greatest worry was that he would put a lot of effort into his job, wouldn't be recognized for his accomplishments, and would then be forgotten as the business grew. "That's a lot of risk, effort, and hard work, with a very low chance of reward," Joe exclaimed with a look of almost fear in his face.

What Will It Take?

What will it take to become an effective leader for probably the most diverse labor pool in the history of the world? What type of company leadership model will capture the hearts of today's employees? How do we become the company that attracts and retains the best talent and turns them into loyal employees who absolutely love what they do?

SINCERELY BE INTERESTED IN YOUR EMPLOYEES' LIVES

You must first realize that a lot of employees might be going through something negative in their lives. Others are broken and living in toxic relationships. Many are carrying with them life's hurts, struggles, and baggage. Inevitably they bring all this adversity to work with them. Those personal problems bring about challenges that management, whether they want to or not, must address, challenges that will interfere with productivity and the tasks that need to be completed.

The negatives in a person's life don't make them a bad employee, just an employee who needs special attention. Managers should get busy realizing what the issues are and repairing them, rather than recycling them out and exchanging them for a new employee. Most of the time, firing a person doesn't fix anything because the person you terminate will be replaced with someone else who may also have personal issues. The issues may be the same, similar, or totally different, but there will be personal problems.

Most managers never know what life issues one of their employees is going through. They don't know the full story and the impact those issues are having on the person. What you can know is that most people are just doing the best they can—the best not only when they are off work, but also when they are on the clock.

The average person does not want to be a failure. Most people have a desire to perform well at work and genuinely want to succeed. No one wants to be written up at work and certainly not fired. Most people have the best intentions to succeed at their job. Sometimes, however, those good intentions aren't good enough to avoid being derailed by distractions in their personal life.

YOUR RESPONSIBILITY

As a manager, your job is to engage with and motivate your employees to deliver outstanding performance. You're expected to oversee workplaces of productivity and profitability. When you see a problem with an employee, you will likely address it and immediately see the employee make positive changes in their performance.

This is generally how it works in business. The manager notices an employee's work performance is substandard and does something to correct it. Notice I said, "The manager notices"! Most employee problems in the workplace go unnoticed. There may be all sorts of issues with your employees that go completely unnoticed. Usually, problems are not being discovered because the supervisor isn't doing a good job at managing. After all, most people do their best to do their best when their supervisor is around. They probably even pour it on and work extra hard when he is around! Most of the underperformance occurs when you are not present, when employees can get by with doing the least amount of work.

> **Three employees were working at coke sintering dust screening locations at one of the nation's largest steel mills. "Coke" is the product derived from low-ash and low-sulfur bituminous coal used in blast furnaces at steel mills. Two of the employees drove large payloaders, and a third employee operated the**

screening plant. The employees in the payloaders would scoop up various amounts of coke out of a pile with their machines and dump it into a hopper. The hopper would vibrate and separate the larger pieces of coke from the finer coke dust. The finer coke dust would be moved away from the hopper via an elevated conveyer belt.

Three or four locations ran twenty-four hours a day, consisting of two twelve-hour shifts. Depending on the time of year, each shift operated in three to five hours of darkness, which required the workers to use the headlights on their payloaders. The mill rules mandated that all vehicles and equipment utilize their headlights from dusk until dawn. This also meant the supervisor had to use his headlights when driving around.

The employees would know if their supervisor was approaching during the night because they could see his headlights approaching their work location. The supervisor knew his employees were working hard at nighttime because he could see from his office the payloader's headlights moving around. Or could he?

On both shifts, two highly paid heavy equipment operators were rolling around for three-to-five hours of their night shift with empty payloader buckets. They would act as if they were scooping up coke, drive over to the hopper, and pretend to empty their buckets of coke into the hopper. Not only were these employees paid hourly, but they were paid time and half for anything over eight hours a day. They were also paid double time on Saturdays and Sundays and triple time on holidays. This practice had been going on for decades, costing the company thousands of hours of pay for nothing, not to mention other costs for running and maintaining the equipment.

The third employee operating the screening plant had to grease the fittings on the machine and conveyor belts at the beginning of his shift and again halfway through his shift. The process took an hour each time, time during which the payloader operators were not able to work. It added an additional two hours per shift of doing nothing to the already three-to-five hours of empty bucket work. Their supervisor had no idea what was going on.

When you see a problem and correct the issue, you may see immediate improvement, but what you don't see is what happens when you leave. Many people go right back to doing what they were doing before. It is human nature to take the path of least resistance—to do what is easy, especially when their supervisor is not around to ensure that demands are complied with, when no one is there to manage them with fear and threats.

If problems are not handled correctly, improvement will likely be short lived. If a person changes their behavior out of fear, then the situation wasn't handled correctly. Real, lasting change won't occur because employees fear they are going to get into trouble. A threat doesn't inspire anyone to do better. It does not bring about a sincere desire in an employee's heart to work harder and do better.

Incorrect management won't spawn valuable change, but rather change brought about only by micromanaging employees. This sort of change kicks in when you're present but evaporates as soon as you leave. Employees who only perform optimally when you're around won't truly be productive for your company. Combined with the time you'll spend spying on them and their not being truly committed, the cost to your company will be a greater loss of revenue!

You desire change! How should you handle a problem correctly, so it results in the true change you desire as a leader? Behavioral changes coming from within the person rather than from the manager's "getting after them" is the desired goal. Change from within would be much better than "supposed" employee behavioral changes coupled with anger and resentment towards you or your company. What you should want and what will bring about lasting change is for employees to have a sincere desire to change—a desire to change for the right reasons. Those right reasons will present themselves when employees embrace the fact that you truly love them and desire what's best for them. This knowledge will cause them to want to change and make positive changes on their own.

Make Them Believers

Most employees couldn't possibly believe that the managers at their company sincerely care about them. To show them you care about them won't be an easy task, and it probably won't happen quickly. It will take time to develop a sincere relationship. Once it takes hold and they fully understand that you genuinely care about them, positive change will usually occur quickly and almost effortlessly.

This relationship building may seem like a whole lot of hard work. It is, but it can be made easier if you understand that the only person you can truly change is yourself and no one else. That statement might not be sitting well with you. As a manager, you want to change people for a better work outcome; you desire to get them to do things your way.

How do you interact with your employees to get them to make the decision to change on their own without your putting a lot of pressure on them and exercising your authority as their manager? What kind of interaction would compel payloader operators to perform their job duties even when it was dark out and their shift supervisor couldn't sneak up on them? Let's see how one manager, Barry, won the heart of one of his employees:

Natalie rushed into the employee entrance. She was late, and it wasn't the first time. The look of distress on her face, combined with her red eyes and smeared make-up immediately conveyed something was awry. "I know. I am late again. I'm so sorry. I had a family issue this morning," she apologized. Her manager, Barry, called her into his office. Natalie knew this was not the first time she had been late for work. As she walked into Barry's office, she was expecting to be written up and maybe even fired.

Barry utilized the training he had received from his appreciative inquiry course and immediately began to address all of the positive contributions Natalie made at work. She had been at the company for eight years, and the first five years had yielded stellar performance reviews. In those early years, she had received regular raises, bonuses, and even a promotion. She was still doing a decent job, but her performance was substandard compared to past years.

He praised her for several positives and then took things a step further. Barry began, "Natalie, I don't want to be too personal, but here at ABC Company we truly care about our employees. I truly care about all our employees. Can you share with me what is going on? I promise to keep it confidential. I promise I won't judge you and will only use the information you share to help you."

Natalie began to weep. Her tears were flowing not only because of what she was about to share, but also because she felt Barry and the company she was working for took a sincere interest in her. Natalie shared that her husband of ten years, Brock, had been unable to work for over three years due to health problems. Brock had been a hard worker and always provided for his family. He had always been a wonderful and loving husband and father.

He was working as a painter and broke his back when he fell off a ladder. He was in a lot of pain and had a couple of back surgeries. His doctors had prescribed a variety of opioids for pain and some other medications to help him sleep. Soon Natalie realized her husband had become addicted to the narcotics that had been meant to help him. He found himself needing more pills than prescribed, and the doctors not only wouldn't increase his dosage, but they also ended up cutting him off completely.

Brock had become verbally and sometimes physically abusive. He was spending most of Natalie's paycheck buying street drugs. This wasn't leaving enough money to cover their mortgage, car payments, and other miscellaneous bills. Natalie was stressed, concerned about the man she dearly loved, the thought of their house being foreclosed on and the possibility of their automobiles being repossessed. Everything combined was having a negative effect on her personal and professional life. She wasn't getting enough sleep, causing her to often be late to work. When at work, her mind constantly wandered about her personal problems. She was barely productive.

What did Barry do corporately? He gave her some paid time off to work on her personal problems. He activated an employee assistance program the company had in place to give her an interest-free loan to bring her mortgage and auto loans current. Barry was able to get her husband Brock into a detox and addiction program that partnered with the company. Their services were offered at a sliding scale, and the company agreed to pick up any costs Natalie and Brock could not afford. He also enrolled both of them into the company's online personal finance program.

What did Barry do personally? He and his wife

befriended Natalie and Brock. They had them over for dinners and did other non-work-related activities with them. Barry and his wife both made themselves available for phone calls when Natalie or Brock needed someone to talk to. Basically, Barry and his wife decided to love Natalie and her husband unconditionally. They did so without judgment and did so confidentially. Whatever was shared with them stayed with them. Nothing relayed off the clock was noted in any personnel files or conveyed to upper management.

What was the result? Over time and with treatment, Brock was able to beat his addiction. He and Natalie were able to get their bills under control, follow a budget, and start saving money. Natalie was never late for work again, and her job performance reached unprecedented heights. She is still with the company and up for promotion at the time this chapter is being written. Due to Brock's injuries, he was never able to return to painting or any other physical work. The company ended up hiring him to work as a courier, and he has turned into a stellar employee.

Both Natalie and Brock absolutely love their jobs, are loyal company employees, and are both committed for life. The company and management took a sincere interest in them in and out of work. Management wasn't just a boss, but a human being who saw an employee and her spouse as fellow human beings—human beings who needed a little help. Barry and his wife "did life" with Natalie and Brock. This unconditional love saved a marriage and a family, as well as created a valuable employee. The same unconditional love was also invested in the husband of an employee, helped salvage his life, and eventually converted him into a valued employee.

If that approach is not an example of positively affecting more than the workplace, I don't know what is! It affected a husband and wife, their family, and no doubt the community around them. How did it benefit the community? Brock was no longer an addict running around on the streets, which lowered the possibility of potential crime and the need for police intervention. Natalie and Brock's house wasn't foreclosed on, and their automobiles were not repossessed. A rundown, vacant, foreclosed house was not left cluttering the neighborhood, waiting to be auctioned off. The auto lenders did not end up taking a loss on the cars they had loaned money on.

The bigger picture is that the family wasn't broken apart. Natalie did not become a single mother, forced to work two jobs to support herself and her children. The children did not become fatherless, a condition that puts children at great risk. Fatherless children are seven times more likely to become pregnant as teens, more likely to have behavioral problems, and more likely to experience abuse and neglect. They are more likely to abuse drugs and alcohol, more likely to engage in criminal activity, more likely to go to prison, and two times more likely to drop out of school.

Barry and his company may very well have kept Brock out of prison and saved Natalie and Brock's children from a life of living on the wrong side of the statistics concerning fatherless children. Imagine if each year the majority of companies in America were able to help several employees' families in a similar way. Wouldn't it be game changer for our communities and families?

UNCOMPLICATED AND UNCONDITIONAL

W E TEND TO view people, conversations, and situations through complicated lenses. We complicate relationships and interactions with people with our preconceived notions. We prejudge people based on a variety of self-created, stereotypical checklists. These checklists are usually based on something we have heard or our limited experiences. Prejudging happens very quickly when people meet each other for the first time. All parties immediately begin to size each other up and collect just enough data about each other to start the analyzation process. After compiling their dossier, they shuffle each other into a category.

The saying should not be "First impressions last a lifetime," but "First perceptions ruin possibilities." Often before a manager meets a new employee, he has looked at the resume and formed a preconceived image as to who that person is. Then when the manager meets the potential employee, in the first 30 to 60 seconds, the manager tries to analyze the potential employee and then categorize him like a library book. Then the manager places the potential employee on a shelf, identified by a genre, labeled with a Dewey Decimal Classification, all without ever taking the time to learn that person's story. Most managers never bother to check out the employee's table of contents or read each chapter that makes up who they are!

WHAT IS REALLY LEARNED?

What can we truly learn about someone in that 30- to 60-second first impression? In most cases, nothing much at all. The reality is that we can't really learn anything about a person—who they truly are—in a minute or less. You can't learn a lot about a person in hours, a few days, a week, or even a month. Sadly, that is exactly how most people make their decision about others—what they think they have learned in 60 seconds.

When one person meets another person for the first time, they go through their first impression, complicated lens checklist. Generally, the checklist looks something like this, with some additions and some subtractions:

1. What's their physical appearance like: height, weight, color, beautiful, average, ugly, etc.?
2. How do they communicate: too soft, too loud, too fast, too slow, too lengthy, mumbling, speaking with arrogance, speaking with no confidence, etc.?
3. What's their personality like: introverted, extroverted, thinker, communicator, etc.?
4. What does their body language say about them: guarded, open, coordinated, clumsy, no swagger,

too much swagger, confident, insecure, etc.?

5. How do they dress: the type of outfit worn, the cost and quality of the apparel, the appropriateness of what they are wearing, the way their clothes fit, whether their outfit is clean or dirty, etc.?

6. What are their mannerisms like: polite, confident, humble, arrogant, snobby, kind, modest, etc.?

7. What do they drive: family car, sports car, luxury car, smart car, junker, etc.?

8. What part of town do they live in: the right or wrong side of the tracks, city or country, suburbs, etc.

9. What is their belief system: Christianity, Judaism, Taoism, Hinduism, Buddhism, Islam, Confucianism, atheist, agnostic, etc.?

10. What's their political affiliation? Republican, Democrat, Libertarian, independent, etc.?

11. What's their culture: customs, laws, dress, social standards, humor, diet, religious beliefs, tradition, etc.?

And the checklist could go on and on. So much information could be listed, yet no list comes close to scratching the surface of who a person really is. It doesn't reveal a tenth of a person's past or present state. Their story can never be gathered by checking boxes. Then there's the infinite number of other unique things about people that can be added to the above list. Does all of that seem a tad daunting? Overwhelming? It shouldn't be a negative, but a positive. It should excite you! The relationships you are about to begin building with your employees will never get stale. There's so much to learn and so much to bond over.

Once we gather up a bunch of information from the checklist, we analyze, categorize, and make a quick judgment on who the person is. We think we have them all figured out and we can't possibly be wrong. In almost every case, we are totally wrong!

A man named Joe worked at a company I was doing consulting work for. Everyone complained that he talked too loudly and was always seeking attention. His coworkers shunned him, gossiped about him, and avoided interacting with him

Why was Joe acting the way he did? Was it because he was a blowhard consciously seeking attention? Or was he hard of hearing? Or maybe he was seeking attention, but he was doing it subconsciously. Maybe in his entire life, he had never experienced unconditional love.

I have employed a few Joes in my life. One man who used to work for me always wanted to be the center of attention. I knew there was a reason behind it, but I did not find out what the reason was until his dad, who lived in another state, passed away. When I heard the news, I spoke with him about giving him some extended time off. He immediately refused the offer. He said he couldn't afford to travel to attend the funeral. I suspected that was not true but offered to pay for his travel and hotel expenses. He refused that offer too.

He finally shared his story. His dad had never paid any attention to him when he was growing up. He missed every one of his birthdays, every game he

played, and even his graduation ceremony. That lack of attention while growing up had caused him to always be seeking what he never received as a child. When people do not receive what they desperately need to grow and flourish as children, they often chase it their entire life.

Another company I did some work for employed a man named Jerome. Everyone that worked with him labeled him a pathological liar. They took issue with the way he exaggerated and lied all the time, not just about things at work but about everything. It was almost like he believed every lie he told and lived in a fabricated fantasy world. He would even lie about situations that everyone knew the truth about.

Why would anyone act that way? Although everyone wants to be accepted by their peers and feel validated, the average person does not go to great lengths to lie and make up stories to become part of the group. A person who does that must have some deep-seated hurts that cause them to go overboard to gain acceptance and validation. It's hard to get such a person to admit what the real issues are and stop the lying and exaggerating.

A man who recently stopped working for me was just like Jerome. He would lie about everything. The stories he told were the types of yarns so outlandish that no prudent person would ever believe them. He bragged that he owned a half-million-dollar home, but everyone knew he lived in an average home located in an area known for crime and violence. He bragged that he paid $90,000 for his truck. Everyone knew that this was another one of his outrageous tales since another coworker had just paid $40,000 for a truck of the exact same year, make, and model.

I tried to find out the underlying cause to his problem. I attempted to get to know him, help him, and mentor him, but he kept his wall battle-ready and extra-high. I have a few guesses as to what the problem might have been. I can't be for sure, so I won't speculate. Doing so would cause me to be judgmental without knowing all the facts. I never learned the why and was never able to have a breakthrough with him. Sadly, he moved on without letting me help him.

A coworker could be talking loudly because he has a hearing problem. A new employee might be talking very fast because he or she is nervous about starting a new job. Someone might be walking funny because they are nervous or anxious over meeting their new manager and coworkers. Someone else might seem arrogant, but the real reason for their behavior might be that they are overcompensating for their shyness by trying hard to appear confident.

Another person may be impossible to work with because they are always angry and confrontational. This person may actually be scared and feel bad about being the type of person they are. That is why they are always angry and adversarial. There's always a reason. We need to make sure that we get it right by taking time to truly get to know people.

Take Your Time

Accurately learning about a person isn't something that happens quickly. It occurs over months, years, decades, and even a lifetime. In order to achieve a meaningful relationship, "the accurately learning about a person" component also must transpire. You cannot have one without the other. Those two components, learning and relationship, must be present and constantly growing to foster success in ways most people can never imagine.

The learning also needs to work both ways. The leader must begin to learn things about the employee, and the employee needs to start learning about the leader. The ebb and flow of the knowledge exchange and the relationship development cause both to stimulate and build upon each other. The result is mutual growth between the individuals. Growth through knowledge and relationship is not an overnight event, but rather an extended endeavor that takes time and effort.

A lifetime timeline and intentional investment are wonderful components because they both facilitate the goal: forming deep-rooted, sincere relationships. Relationships should edify both the employees and the leaders. Both in business and in life, relationships should allow all parties to invest in one another as they are "doing life" together. Such investment brings about positive changes not only in our company, but also in our personal lives and in the communities we live and work in. When your business can make a beneficial impact in all three areas, it can change the world in which you live, making the people that reside around us better citizens.

As business owners, it's a plan where everyone wins. Your community will be better for it, which will better the populace. Those that live, work, and grow the economy through commerce will greatly benefit. It makes them better customers and helps to make your business more successful and profitable. This allows for company growth that permits your business to invest in people and the community even more.

UNCOMPLICATE YOUR LENS

Leaders need to uncomplicate the lens through which they view those around them. They need to see people in an unfiltered way that doesn't immediately cloud their ability to lead and mentor a person. Once you taint your thoughts and form opinions about someone, it is hard to move past what you are sure is true. Those preconceived ideas handicap you as a leader. For the employee, it lessens their chance of becoming a better employee.

View them right where they are without any assumptions or prejudice. In the hiring process there is no need to begin to identify strengths and weaknesses if they seem to be a good fit for your company. That time will come later. It's not the time to start trying to fix someone, modify their behavior, or put them on a performance improvement plan. It's time to look at them without expectations, judgment, or stereotypical preconceived thoughts and ideas.

Uncomplicating your view of your employees allows you to identify your commonalities and your differences. You will learn which employees have a story that is similar to yours, different than yours, or more or less complicated than yours. You may discover how they have been raised and why they behave the way they do. Learning about your employees can be an entirely positive experience for both of you if you allow it to lead to relationship building.

When you discover mutual similarities that you have with a person, there is somewhat of an instant bonding that occurs between the two of you. That bonding will allow you to relate to them easier. Differences are an excellent opportunity to explore and get to know a person more.

During the first days of employment, accept the flaws, the mistakes, and the annoying habits. It should not be a time of trying to fix and correct your employees. It is a time to build meaningful relationships. Doing so makes the behavioral changes you want to see easier. It will bring about willful changes rather than change resulting from fear. The result will be that your employees will want to change out of love and loyalty to you. They will want to perform better and be more productive, just as much as you want them to.

Unconditional Love

Can a leader love the employees that work for them? Yes! Can a leader love unconditionally? Absolutely, but it can be difficult. You'll need to move from looking at failures, problems, and deficiencies to instead concentrating on strengths and successes. Recognizing the strengths and values of what works, as opposed to what is wrong, will transform employees, resulting in the transformation of your organization.

Be a leader that isn't negative and critical of your staff. Instead show them unconditional love, even when they mess up. When they see that you are looking at their positives instead of their errors, they will desire to be a better employee and utilize their gifts while trying to avoid making mistakes.

Always be encouraging, uplifting, and empowering. Having positive interactions and conversations with them will help to move them down a positive path. Being positive instead of negative will help them to overcome their own negativity. That positive outlook will cause them to be happier about coming to work and lead them to enjoy being there. They will work harder, achieve their goals, and be more productive.

When you reshape a person's thoughts concerning how they see the company and their role in it, you change the company, its culture, and its environment.

Transparency

The Obstacles of Building Relationships

Building relationships takes a lot of effort, and often there is little or no reward. Many people don't want to invest a lot of effort into the development of relationships they feel probably won't work out. More and more, relationships are forged on the screens of social media and through the facelessness of texting. What is absent from those technological screens is emotion, feelings, and physical and verbal interaction. Others aren't able to go very far into another person's real life, which is hidden by their offline world. People seem to be alright with that, and they seemingly aren't interested in seeing past the virtual world of their internet acquaintances.

Getting to know people and developing relationships can be difficult. Most people truly desire relationships and even yearn to have them. Yet even though the appetite and longing to get to know others exists, people avoid doing so. They stop themselves from pursuing intimacy before the quest to develop relationships even begins. Often individuals that might be a candidate for a relationship are pushed away. Sometimes even the possibility of a relationship is sabotaged, either consciously or subconsciously.

THE LENS OF THE PAST

Relational fear is derived from a variety of reasons, based on events that have occurred in a person's past. Most people tend to filter all things through the lens of their past. These past experiences are viewed as predictors of future relationships and experiences. They raise red flags in a person's mind, and fear sets in. The person doesn't want to experience a similar hurtful outcome to one they experienced in a former relationship.

People bring past pains, problems, and even positive experiences into their present. Sadly, the good is often overridden by the bad because the wounds experienced were extremely painful, deeply personal, and not easily forgotten. Being used, abused, discarded, marginalized, and undervalued are stings that can last a lifetime. It is hard to recover when divorce, familial hurts, lost friendships, relationship let downs, and other wounds occur. When the same types of injuries are repeated over and over, it is even harder to rebound. People can't recover from pain, injury, and disappointment when they are anticipating the reoccurrence of such traumas.

BATTLE-READY EMOTIONAL WALLS

Employees with painful baggage build emotional walls to protect themselves from being hurt again. Walls keep them from initiating real interaction and protect them from people who launch a bid at a relationship. Walls stifle the excitement of getting to know new people and keep interaction with others to a minimum. Walls announce, "Taking this chance is not worth it," "Don't trust anyone," "It'll eventually go bad," and "You're better off not engaging with others." Choosing to take a much safer path, the wall builder keeps others at distances that exclude any possibility of a relationship and allow him to avoid getting to know others.

MANAGEMENT TRANSPARENCY

Management transparency allows your staff to see that you are not perfect. It gives them permission to view your past hurts and disappointments. It lets them view you as human—a human with not only strengths and positives, but also faults, insecurities, and disappointments. Your staff can relate to you better and you with them when they view the real you.

"Pretty scary!" you might declare. You are probably thinking that if your employees see you as fallible, they won't respect you, that they will view you as weak or unworthy to lead. Never let them see you sweat!

YOU DON'T HAVE THEM FOOLED!

They already know you're not perfect! They have a list of things they think you are wrong about. Your company is probably filled with laughter and snickering about your flaws and mistakes. Most of the people you have working for you have uttered at least once, "You have no idea what you're doing. I could do your job much better than you can." Often, they feel leaders are overpaid for doing nothing. Not only do they find fault with management, but they make often make up things that don't even exist.

I was surprised by an assumption that one of the employees at my residential and commercial development company made about me. He felt comfortable sharing his thoughts about me because of the environment of company transparency I had worked so hard to develop. The transparency in my companies works both ways, so I was not surprised or offended by what he stated. He said I was just like all of the other business owners he had worked for in the past because I didn't do much of anything except drive around in my company truck, talk on my cell phone, and go to business lunches. He did admit that I probably sent a few emails when I was in my office and sometimes showed up to check on my crews.

I wasn't offended. In fact, I was amused. I viewed his opinion as a training opportunity and explained to him exactly what duties my role entails. I not only verbalized it, but I also had him spend a few days with me in my world. He got to personally see the plethora of phone calls I receive from contractors, realtors, insurance companies, title companies, building inspectors, lenders, and employees from the various companies I own.

For three days, he witnessed me putting out fires, problem solving, battling with suppliers, putting together deals that kept him and others employed, and answering and sending hundreds of emails and texts every few days. He found out that my day begins at 4 a.m. and often ends close to midnight. At the end of his "ride along" with me, the man who felt I didn't do much of anything was begging to get back to his 8 to 4 labor position.

Through the culture of transparency, he was able to watch me succeed and watch me fail, watch me do things right and watch me make mistakes. My stressful moments, my frustration, my highs, and my lows were all laid out for him to view. He saw the good, the bad, and the ugly in the role I hold at the company, as well as in my personal life. He thanked me for showing him my business and personal side, along with the many tasks I handled every day that he did not know about.

Beginning Wall Demolition

Acting as if you are some sort of infallible super-leader does not impress anyone. It is seen as arrogant, unreal, insecure, and desperately hiding who you truly are. Complete transparency demonstrates to your employees that you're confident in your flawed skin. It shows you are consciously aware of your imperfection, but you don't feel threatened about that knowledge; you are comfortable feeling less important so others can feel more important and more valued.

When leaders are transparent with their employees, it starts the process of chiseling away at walls. The employees realize that management has switched the focus from hidden leaders in perfect palaces to open and transparent members of the "boots on the ground" team. Transparency will revolutionize employee loyalty and motivation, as well as help them to catch the vision of the company. It is a slow process, and people grow and become better employees at different timelines and levels. It isn't easy, but the result will be well worth all of the hard work.

It Starts with You

Transparency ultimately starts with you. Don't hide who you are. That includes your failures, as well as your successes.

Transparency shows your weaknesses, fears, strengths, and confidence. Don't be afraid to share your past, present, and future with your employees. Once they see that your walls have been razed and you are not afraid to be transparent, they will begin to do the same.

RELATIONAL RESULTS

Relationally, being transparent will ultimately result in your learning information about your employees that you never knew. They will learn things about you too. This will help you to understand each other better and allow you to better relate to one another. I have found out things about people both professionally and personally that I never would have learned if I had not utilized transparency in our relationships. Once they saw that I was not afraid to let my guard down and reveal the real me, they responded equally with their own transparency.

KNOWLEDGE TRULY IS POWER

I have employed many people, both in America and globally. No matter where people are from, they all have a story. Borders don't change the fact that people have past trauma, emotional baggage, and often present struggles. All humans have mountains and valleys in their lives. Everyone has hurts and fears, triumphs and dreams.

As a leader, when you go through the process of building meaningful relationships with your people, you will learn a plethora of information about them. You will hear all kinds of stories and possibly shocking information. Don't judge the person and don't react negatively. Just listen sincerely with great interest to what they share. Allow them to speak freely, absent of interruption or pressure. As they open up, the information you gather will help you to understand what motivates them, how they learn, and what roles and job duties would be their best fit. You will gain insight about what makes them who they are and learn their heartfelt needs.

Yes, knowledge is power. The knowledge you discover through relationship building does give you power—the power to help your employees grow and become successful both professionally and personally. This power enables you to mentor and guide them in ways they relate to best, to understand how they receive and perceive correction, and to know what style of training moves them to make the performance changes you desire.

What I Learned in Transparent Relationships

CASE STUDY ONE

One employee transparently shared with me that he had been raised in multiple foster homes during his childhood and that he had been verbally, emotionally, physically, and sexually abused by his biological parents and even by some of his foster parents. When he was in sixth grade, he was at a local carnival. Some older boys began to bully him. They dragged him into a field behind the church that was hosting the event and tried to force feed him a garter snake tail first. He was mercilessly bullied at school from kindergarten until he graduated from high school.

He told me that besides his psychiatrist, I was the only person he felt comfortable sharing his past with. I listened with a keen interest and never judged him for his past. I befriended him and developed a lifetime relationship with him. Throughout our relationship, I told him that the trauma he had endured from his parents and foster parents had conditioned him to believe that what was happening was normal behavior. Those years of abuse set him up to be targeted by other abusers. Over the years, I was able to help him develop self-confidence and refuse to allow others to bully him.

In time, I was able help him overcome the grim past that had made up most of his preadult life. He became an exemplary employee that any company would be pleased to employ for a lifetime. However, he did not work for me for a lifetime but resigned a few years after I hired him. You might be thinking, What a waste of time, money and energy!

Not at all. He went on to start a very successful small business, marry, and have two beautiful children. He became a productive member of society, employed several people at his business, and paid forward to others the love and patience I had given him. It was a win for my company, a win for the local community, a win for him, and a win for mankind!

CASE STUDY TWO

One day a young woman who worked for me began

to weep uncontrollably. She revealed that she had spent the preceding twelve years of her marriage being physically abused almost daily by her husband. He would beat her, spit in her face, and choke her constantly. She chose what clothes to wear and what makeup to use to best cover her bruises. She told me that although she was financially dependent on him, she was leaving him because she did not want her ten-year-old daughter to think it was alright to be treated that way by a man. After having a discussion with her abusive husband and helping her financially, she was able to get out of her situation.

I was able to be there for her and help her make many changes in her life. She became one of the best employees on my staff and thrived while working for me. She went on to thrive as a middle manager of a large company and eventually marry a man that respected her. Her greatest joy was to see her daughter grow up in a home where everyone was loved and valued unconditionally. Another employee lost? Maybe. But the new company she went to work for began using my company's services. In time, several of their customers also became my customers. I built some great business relationships because of taking the time to build that relationship with my employee.

CASE STUDY THREE

Another man who worked for me had grown up in a tumultuous home. His parents were both addicts, but not the back-alley type of addicts most people think of when they see the word addict. There was no shooting up of drugs with a dirty needle or living high and homeless on the street. With his dad it was pills and alcohol, and with his mom it was just pills. They were not buying their pills from some street dealer but procured them the legal way, from doctors. They both functioned quite well and were successful in their careers. Both were verbally abusive to him and also to each other. On paydays, his mom would go from bar to bar, trying to retrieve his dad's paycheck before he spent the bill money on booze. A few nights a week, his dad wouldn't come home, and his mom would load him into the car and drive around to multiple houses where various women lived, trying to find him. Often his dad would come home and beat him, his mom, or both of them. If there was not physical fighting, there was arguing, and it was never just a disagreement, but screaming, yelling, and threats of violence, with a lot of cursing mixed in.

Nothing he did was ever good enough. A grade of A- was not satisfactory because it was not an A+, not 100% perfect. They told him he was dumb and would never be smart enough to please them, and they expressed that regularly. His room was never clean enough. His chores were never good enough. The list of failures went on and on. When he tried to play sports, his dad made fun of him for being clumsy and not athletic, even though his dad never spent one

———

minute playing any sport with him. He told him he wasn't tough enough or man enough to play sports. He called him a pansy, made homosexual slurs, and used other demeaning words that destroyed his confidence. His dad used to tell him he would never find a girl to date him because girls were attracted to real men.

His mom also treated him in a demeaning way. She told him he would never amount to anything and that he'd be lucky to graduate from high school. She predicted that he might be able to get a job as a "stinky" garbage man if he didn't end up in prison.

He cannot remember either of them ever saying, "I love you," hugging him, or showing any type of affection. He would often observe his friends' loving and supportive parents and how they treated his friends. He wondered why he didn't have that and questioned what he must have done to deserve the home life he had. He started to become angry and bitter.

When this man first began to work for me, he had no confidence and was going nowhere in life. Through transparent leadership and other leadership skills taught in this book, I was able to help him be transformed into a confident employee. He began to make plans, set goals, and achieve them. He calls me "Pops" to this day and claims I was the dad he never had.

Transparency should be one of the values your company strives to maintain. Leadership deprived of transparency is

———

probably one of the biggest culprits of ineffective and unprofitable businesses. A company with leadership transparency will develop better teams, be more engaged with employees, and help lower employee turnover rates. It causes managers to be better leaders, listeners, and motivators, and it holds leaders accountable not only to company shareholders and their fellow leaders, but also to their employees. By building teams that trust upwards and downwards, transparency fosters an organization where everyone can effectively listen and respectfully consider others' opinions, looking past their differences.

This trust and accountability will ignite your staff to appreciate and recognize everyone's contributions, as well as to recognize that there is no competition and no heroes, only successful teams. When the good that is accomplished is for the good of the whole company and not individuals, everyone wins and everyone benefits!

Dealing with Different Types of Employees

A S A LEADER, you may encounter many different types of employees. Plenty of factors mold a person's personality, behavior, and outlook on life. Some of those factors are culture, education, heredity, health, environment, experiences, and maturity. Leaders must discover how to deal with many different and unique types of employees. In this chapter, I am going to highlight a small group of personalities. If you are interested in learning how to deal with even more personalities, please visit my company's website at www.traininglion.com for further training on dealing with various types of employees.

Through careful mentoring, you can change some things about your employees for the better. Just know that you will never be able to change who they are completely. You can work to understand them better. You can learn the best ways to lead them by discovering what motivates them. Identifying their strengths and weaknesses will help you manage them. Magnifying and building upon their strengths, while not focusing on and minimizing their faults, will garner the positive results you desire.

Any conversation or corrective action taken needs to take place privately, and the interaction should be nonconfrontational, positive, and kind. Be courteous, friendly, and gracious always, but even more so during these kinds of conversations. The employee should leave the meeting feeling that the mentoring you provided was mostly for their benefit and that your desire was to help them do better, rather than being punitive. If you learn to understand that all negative behavior comes from past and present hurts and experiences, you can mentor your staff with both empathy and sympathy.

THE BELLYACHER

Dealing with a chronic complainer can be trying at best and "pull-your-hair-out" frustrating at worst. To interact with them properly, you must understand them as best you can. People complain about things for a variety of reasons. Sometimes they do it to get noticed or for attention. They may be trying to make someone else look bad to benefit themselves. To do so, they do not have to say a word about themselves; instead they can point out all of the negatives about their coworkers. Complaining about the difficulty of a task that's been assigned may be a way of removing personal accountability or excusing deficiencies in their performance.

You need to take the reins when dealing with a complainer. Determine if their complaint is valid. If it is, come up with a solution that fixes the issue. Ask them for their input on how they would correct the issue if they were in charge. If their idea works or if part of it does, implementing it will make the employee feel valued. If it is an invalid complaint, redirect the discussion to something else or explain why it truly isn't an issue. Lastly, don't be afraid to constructively point out that they constantly complain. Compile a detailed list of all their past and present complaints and kindly share the list with them. Be prepared to educate them on how their complaining negatively affects their coworkers, the company atmosphere, and operations in general.

THE SQUEALER

I have employed more than one person who loved to run to me and share information about other employees. Squealers are easy to identify; they will be eagerly waiting for a moment alone with you to snitch on one their coworkers. They'll start the conversation with, "I hate to tell you this..."; "I don't want to be the bearer of bad news..."; or "I think you should know...." You'll be amazed at how much more they know about your staff than you do.

The squealer will spend lots of time identifying co-workers' errors, often making notes, sometimes mentally and sometimes written, about everyone around them. They might even build a detailed dossier on each one of them. Once they collect enough damaging info on someone, you'll always hear about it in great detail.

Someone's sharing info about one of your employees isn't always bad. It can be a useful tool for identifying issues that can be used as training opportunities. It depends on the reason the info is being shared. It's bad if it's being done to get in management's good graces, to look better than a colleague, or to cover up one's own inefficiencies. It's alright if it's a safety issue, the company is being hurt, or company policy is being violated.

Other factors are the frequency of the sharing and whether the information is accurate. Is what you are being told made up or embellished? Or is it factual and needs to be addressed? If an employee occasionally informs you about something going on, it's acceptable. If an employee is living a constant "squealer's lifestyle" by spending lots of time squealing, it is unacceptable. The continual tattling will severely undermine team cohesiveness and hurt interoffice relationships. It will damage morale and interfere with productivity.

You need to educate a squealer about what is important for you to know and what isn't. If another employee comes in seven minutes late one day, you don't need to hear about. It's unnecessary for them to tell you if someone took a longer lunch than is allowed. Let them know you do want to hear about the actions that are serious threats to the company. Sexual harassment and other injustices, theft, fraud, company sabotage, bullying, threats of violence, and other like actions should always be immediately reported.

THE GOSSIPER

First make sure your company has a detailed company policy to which you can reference the offending employee. Also realize that gossip in the workplace is always going to occur. The problem arises when it becomes disruptive to your organization's operations. This happens when gossip becomes excessive to the point that morale and productivity are negatively affected. When it becomes evident that relationships between coworkers are being injured and people are having their feelings hurt, the gossiper must be addressed immediately.

Be sure the offending employee understands how the gossip they are engaging in is damaging to their coworkers and the company. Try to get them to imagine how they would feel if they were on the receiving end of the chatter. They need to be made aware that it will be unacceptable if they continue to engage in gossip and that it could lead to further discipline as laid out in your company's handbook.

The Hurt

Everyday life comes with hurts: past hurts, present hurts, or fears of potential future hurts. Some are little, some are big, and some impact a person permanently. The best leaders put their employees first, even over their customers. Your employees are truly one of the most important components keeping your company alive and healthy. You need to pay attention to your employees and learn about hurts they have experienced.

If possible, identify how greatly certain hurts have affected them. You need to be compassionate and careful with the hurt people you lead. Try to help them recover and work through what has hurt them in the past. Help them to learn how to deal with present hurts and how to avoid the fear of future hurts that may never occur. Although hurts will come their way, success or failure is not determined by the hurtful event. Future success is about how they receive the hurt and how they react to it. More important is how they move forward once they experience a hurt. You need to deal with hurt people because those who have been hurt tend to repeatedly hurt those around them. That endless cycle will negatively affect your company more than you can imagine.

WHEN I GET HURT

When I see hurt on the horizon, I say to myself, "Alright, this is going to hurt, so let's get it over with!" I try to understand the reason behind the hurt. Next I look for ways to mitigate the amount of hurt or opportunities to turn it into a positive. I try to determine if the hurt was avoidable so I can dodge a similar hurt in the future. Lastly, I try to learn from the experience, forget about it, and move on. If you can urge your employees closer to that way of thinking, it will transform the way they are affected by their hurts. It will change their lives!

Candy seemed to have more hurts than anyone I know. Her entire life was filled with deep hurts committed by family, friends, coworkers, neighbors, church leaders, and church members. Often, she was even hurt by complete strangers. The hurts were so severe and so frequent that she basically became a hermit, spending all her time at home or work. She said she was perfectly happy just to interact with her immediate family.

One day she joked that if there were a worldwide apocalypse that wiped out all the world's population except her and her immediate family, she'd be perfectly content. She said just having her husband and children around would be enough. Some weeks later she shared with me that her husband had moved out and was considering divorcing her. We had several conversations about her circumstances. We both concluded that her life's hurts had finally infected her marriage and family.

I mentored her on my techniques for dealing with hurts and spent some time with her and her husband. They mended their disagreements, he moved back home, and they began to repair their relationship. Candy learned to deal with her past hurts and implemented my methods on handling incoming hurts. Doing so hasn't made her life perfect and she still experiences hurts, but they are less frequent, and her life is much better than it ever was before. She has developed healthy relationships in her community and workplace, and when she experiences hurt, it doesn't hurt as bad, and she moves on quickly.

THE APPLE POLISHER

The apple polisher seems to spend a lot of time doting on the boss. Apple polishers are identified quickly by both management and their coworkers. Some people knowingly engage in apple polishing, insincerely "sucking up" to the boss to garner favor, position, and other benefits. Others see themselves as loyal employees who are devoted to and admire their manager. They never realize they are an apple polisher!

Gently let both types know it is their performance and nothing else that earns promotions and raises. In a subtle way, inform them that all of your team members are equally favored and you're there for all of them. Convince them that no one will be treated better than anyone else. Never allow an apple polisher to become your favored employee. Doing so will destroy the confidence and zeal with which your team operates. Treat everyone with the same love, respect, and patience.

THE COMPLAINER

The company complainer will bring a cloud of negativity over your entire company. Complainers will infect everyone's perception of the company, cause others to see things negatively, and inspire others to become complainers. Those who don't join in the complaining will find themselves exhausted by the constant complaining going on around them. Having one or more complainers working for you can cause productivity to grind to a halt if the complaining isn't curtailed right away.

Curtailing the complaining will require you to engage the complainer in the midst of an intertwined, working relationship. You can't completely combat complainers unless you get in the trenches with them. Seek their input and let them know they need to come to you with their complaints. Explain that it's you who can address and fix their complaints, that complaining to others won't produce results, and that complaining to their coworkers won't be tolerated.

Set defined expectations with a complainer. One of those expectations is that the constant complaining to those around them is immediately halted. Show them you are the new outlet for their complaints, the one who has the power do something about them, and they are no longer permitted to waste what might be a valid and fixable complaint on people with no authority. Assure them that you will not see their complaints as anything but positive and constructive. Warn them that going to anyone else with their complaints will be viewed as a negative action.

Use your time interacting with them to coach them on replacing their negative complaints with positive recommendations that provide solutions. Teach them to see and appreciate the good that's going on around them, the things the company and staff are doing well. If your complainer continues to engage in behaviors that are harmful to the company, a performance improvement plan (PIP) needs to be deployed. If a PIP doesn't bring about behavioral change, then well documented disciplinary action should be introduced. If that does not induce the changes you desire, then termination may be necessary.

THE INTIMIDATOR

Never allow intimidation or bullying to occur in your company. It must be stopped immediately before it becomes imprinted into your company's culture. Intimidators need to be coached quickly and effectively, with behavioral change occurring rapidly. If intimidation goes on long enough, you will either lose employees or they will lose their zeal for your company. Either loss will negatively impact your company.

I always say to work with and mentor your people until you've exhausted every tool in your tool pouch. Never hastily terminate someone out of frustration or hopelessness, the exception being an employee that is threatening physical harm or violence against any of your management or staff. If this occurs, end their employment and walk them right out of the building.

A few years ago, a distraught company owner named Jack called, asking for my help. His business had once been extremely profitable, but currently it was just limping along. He was experiencing an excessive amount of employee problems, including an employee turnover rate that was though the roof. It was higher than any company I had ever assessed, and his call-off rates were equally mind-boggling. There was absolutely no camaraderie among his staff, and workplace satisfaction was bankrupt. He was ready to close his business and go work a nine-to-five job for someone else.

I scheduled some time to spend a couple of weeks imbedded in his company as a new hire. Jack picked me up at the airport, and we spent about 10 hours together. My questions for him were "When did you first notice a change?" and "What's changed in the running of your company in the last few years?" I also asked him to get me a list of people he hired, fired, or quit.

I wanted him to share with me some details about each employee that had ended up leaving the company.

1.   Why had he hired them?

2. How long did they stay?
3. What was their reason for quitting?
4. What was their performance like at the beginning?
5. Where was their performance level at the midpoint of their employment?
6. How was their performance at the end of their employment?

Specifically, I wanted to know who had managed them and who had worked closely with them.

He provided me with all of the information I requested. Some important answers I picked up on included the following:

1. Jack's dad Eugene had passed away five years earlier.
2. Jack ran the business for about 18 months before bringing on a man named Mitchell as a manager.
3. Every employee that did not work out, eventually quit, or was terminated had been supervised by Mitchell, working on the same crew and shift.
4. Every employee performed extremely well from the day they started until about the halfway mark in their time with the company.
5. At the midpoint of their employment timeline, minor issues began to arise.
6. At the time of their resignation, they had become absolutely useless to the company, and their attitudes were extremely angry and aggressive.

The first three answers raised my antenna as

to what the problem was. I wanted to confirm my thoughts by joining the company and working under Mitchell on his crew. I completed my two weeks of undercover investigating, but I really did not need that much time. By day three, I had determined what most of Jack's company issues were.

On the first day, there were some positives. I found the onboarding process to be smooth and positive. The HR department did an excellent job. They provided me with more than enough company information on company policy, benefits, payroll, and more.

Then Mitchell gave me a facility tour and explained my duties. He appeared to be sizing me up and was not very friendly. Mitchell was a condescending intimidator, who immediately started trying to bully me. I am not the type to be bullied, and when he saw it wasn't working, he became very angry and increased the intimidation.

I was then paired with a man named Eric for on-the-job training. He was also an intimidator and also an apple polisher. Mitchell thoroughly enjoyed Eric's constant apple polishing. He also used Eric as a secondary intimidator to further subjugate staff members.

Both Mitchell and Eric worked hard to cultivate a poisonous work environment that was damaging Jack's business. They encouraged a "high schoolish" type of hazing for new employees, pitted employees against one another, and sowed seeds of distrust among the staff. Several times a day they would angrily confront employees with aggressive words and body language. They would often belittle people and threaten to fire them.

During those two weeks, I got to know the other employees well. They confided in me and shared many of the experiences they had with the company. The company paid well and provided great benefits, so no one wanted to lose their job. The high pay did not lessen their hate for the company. They dreaded coming to work, and all of them were constantly looking for other employment. Everyone worked slowly and was careless with the quality of their work when Mitchell and Eric weren't around. However, when Mitchell and Eric showed up, employees would pick up the pace and work feverishly.

The most revealing facts I learned came from two long-term employees. One was about Jack's dad, Eugene, and how he had run the company when he was alive. Eugene was beloved by every employee, and he had loved his employees back. He had made them feel like family, and they had all affectionately called him Dad. He had invested in their lives, cared about them, and built a strong bond with each of them. He never had to work hard at motivating them because they worked hard out of their love and loyalty for him. From everything I heard, Eugene had been a true *Ace of Hearts* Leader

Secondly, they did not feel like Jack cared about

them at all, at least not the way Eugene had. Jack always seemed distant and uninterested in getting to know the people that worked for him. He never had any lengthy conversations with his employees, never more than just a greeting or a brief talk about something they were working on. He left all the management and employee interaction to Mitchell. He rarely left his office and never managed or assessed Mitchell. He never had an inkling that Mitchell was destroying his company.

Upon sharing my assessment findings with Jack, Mitchell and Eric were both immediately terminated. Jack wasn't surprised the employees felt his dad was a better leader. He knew he didn't interact with them the way his dad had, but he expressed to me that he did love and care for them.

Jack pledged to do better at interacting with his team and determined to work hard at building relationships with them.

EMPLOYEE LONGEVITY IS THE RESULT

A competent leader will learn how to deal with the company's greatest resource—its employees. If you can mold them into long-term, productive employees rather than ones that are constantly leaving, your company will reap the rewards. An untold amount of time, money, and frustration is spent on hiring and training people that don't stay. Try to turn that revolving employee door, where there is a never-ending stream of employees coming and going, into a one-way door. A one-way door is the result of employee longevity. If you can work with your staff in a way that helps to convert them into long-term employees, you will truly be a successful leader!

Interacting — Part 1

INTERACTION IS MUTUALLY beneficial when it allows all parties to freely share their thoughts, feelings, and ideas. Interaction that fosters a sense of value in your employees helps them to see themselves more positively. This allows them to enjoy their work more and causes them to be more motivated and loyal to the company.

Great leaders know how to effectively interact with people. They can easily connect and interact with people from all walks of life, different cultures, and diverse backgrounds. If you want to be a leader who can impact your people, you must learn the art of interacting with others. This chapter will cover some of the basics on how to correctly interact with people, but there is much more to learn. Look for training and other tips on how to properly interact with others.

Be Likeable

Are you a likeable leader or an unlikeable leader? Which type of leader would you rather be? Of the two, would one produce better results than the other? As an employee, would one motivate you more than the other? Which type of person would you want to work for? Do these questions need to be asked? I think we all know the correct answers!

Understand that being a likeable or unlikeable leader shouldn't be confused with being a strong or weak leader. Being likeable doesn't mean that you should be a pushover, where none of your employees respect you. Being likeable does not mean your employees will perceive you as weak and automatically take advantage of you.

LIKED VERSUS POPULAR

Being a leader that is likeable is not the same as being a leader that is popular. Popular leaders can easily become people pleasers, where many decisions are influenced by what the employees think of them. You can't allow your people to dictate your decisions because you are fearful they might stop liking you. When you allow that, your employees are running the company, not you. You become ineffective, unproductive, and no longer needed. You'll be out of a job very quickly!

Being a likeable leader is dispositional, not positional. Your position is the stance you take on company policies, procedures, operations, vision, goals, and everyday matters. Your disposition is how you convey all of those things to your employees. It is not the direction you give, but rather how you give it. Your counseling an employee isn't the issue, but rather the way you deliver the counsel. It isn't the rules you enforce, but the ways you enforce them. You must strive for a balance between making sure everything is being done that the company wants done and disseminating the rules and policies to your people in a positive, motivational, and agreeable way.

You will still need to be a strong leader that effectively supervises your staff, a leader that is not influenced by fears, feelings, and emotions. You must enforce the company guidelines while disciplining and mentoring your people and making wise decisions for the good of the company. You may have to suspend someone for unacceptable behavior. You may even have to fire an employee now and then. That doesn't mean you have to stop loving, caring, and being there for that person. It means you are no longer in an employer/employee relationship. What? How can that be? That can never work! Even crazier, you might terminate an employee and hire them back at some point in the future when they have changed the behavior that caused you to fire them. I can hear you shouting, "No way! Never!" Instead, imagine yourself being a second-chance leader, one who allows for redemption for someone who's willing to change!

I hired a young man to work for me that I will call Will. Will had a bright future when he was growing up. He was good-looking, popular, and a great student with a winsome personality. His smile and laugh were infectious, and I liked him just for that! In high school, he was a talented athlete that excelled at every sport in which he participated. He was especially gifted at baseball and had garnered a full college scholarship after graduation.

Will was also sometimes prone to making bad decisions in an almost self-destructive manner. It was

almost as if he would self-sabotage the good things that were happening in his life. In the middle of his senior year, his girlfriend got pregnant, so he ended up not going to college. He lost his baseball scholarship and part of his youth. He wasn't going to be able to have time to enjoy college or his early adult life. It was time to raise a child and be a family man!

Will started out in an entry-level position at my company. He was a hard worker, learned fast, and became a valued team member right way. Within a few short months, I promoted him to a better paying position with more responsibilities. Soon after that, I promoted him again to a position making around $75,000 a year with a 24/7 company vehicle—not bad for a twenty-something-year-old man in the late 1990s with just a high school diploma.

Things were going well for him. He was making great money, was able to provide for his family, and loved his job. A couple of years later, he started to slip back into some of those besetting self-destructive behaviors. Because I always "do life" with my employees, I picked up on it immediately. He started showing up late for work, calling off, and not answering his phone. He always looked tired and seemed slightly off in his thinking. I had several conversations with him, and after each one, he'd snap back into performing well. Then he'd ease back into not doing well, and I'd have to do some follow-up mentoring.

One day he showed up to get his paycheck. From

my office, I saw a girl in the passenger seat that was not his son's mom. I walked out, spoke with him, and introduced myself to his friend. I told Will I needed to talk with him in my office. I asked him what was going on, and he shared his current story. The girl he was with, Rose, was a stripper that he was seeing on the side. I reminded him that he had a family and that his son was better off growing up in a two-parent home. He let me know he was bored, and that this girl was a lot of fun to hang around with. "Enough fun to lose your family over and get to see your son only every other weekend?" I asked.

He answered, "I don't know. I am just not happy." Things went bad quickly. Rose was an addict. She was hooked on some bad street drugs and was an alcoholic. Will joined her in both of her addictions and eventually became an addict himself. He started calling off a lot, coming in late, and leaving early. He became argumentative and belligerent. I finally had to terminate Will's employment, but I did not stop loving him or trying to be there for him. His addiction caused him to be almost totally unresponsive to communication with me and everyone else.

Over the next few years, Will's life descended into chaos. Rose got pregnant and had a baby boy. Soon after birth, the baby died of SIDS. Drugs and alcohol addictions consumed the lives of both Will and Rose. Will was arrested several times for misdemeanor and felony crimes. One-night Rose died of an overdose.

Will continued even deeper into the world of addiction. After several more arrests, he ended up in prison.

However, Will's story did not end there. I reconnected with Will about two years ago. He had been able to overcome his addictions and was working a steady job. Although his life was slowly getting better, he was living with regrets, guilt, and severe depression. He told me that when he woke up every day in his prison cell, he remembered and rehashed one event: the conversation we had in my office on the day he showed up with Rose. He tearfully told me that he regretted not listening to my advice that day. If he had listened, he was sure he would not have ruined his life.

Since reconnecting, I have helped him get another job, met with him often, and had lots of phone calls with him. He has a steady job that pays well, shows up on time, doesn't call off, and volunteers for overtime. He owns a home and two cars and is in a healthy relationship. Is it just a matter of time before he falls off the wagon again? That is what many people say about addicts. They expect them to go back to their addiction. Who knows? It is not Will's present life, so I won't even entertain the thought.

Terminated and brought back? Will is currently employed at a job he thoroughly enjoys. He is making enough money to support his family and isn't looking to leave the company he works for. Would I hire him again to work for one of my companies? Yes, I would. But before I did, there would be a formal hiring process, my company's normal new-hire drug testing, and a lot of conversations. I would do so very carefully and with a list of conditions, but I would!

COMMUNICATION

People communicate in three ways. Spoken, non-verbal, and written. Spoken communication consists of two components, verbal and paraverbal. Verbal is what is being said and paraverbal is how it is said. Tone, pitch, volume, and tempo dictate the paraverbal part of communication. Non-verbal is basically body language. It's the gestures, facial expressions, and other obvious actions that go along with the words being spoken. The last communication piece is written. Handwritten communication has been taken over by emails, texts, speech-to-text, social media, and other technologies we use to disseminate information.

OUR WORDS

Words are powerful. It has been said that actions speak louder than words. I disagree with that statement. Words are so powerful that they invoke action. Words influence others' thinking, feelings, and emotions. They have the power to calm or agitate. Words can help a person greatly or wound them permanently. They can praise, and they can humiliate. Words can produce laughter or tears and cause people to love or hate. Road rage, fist fights, and wars have been started over words, but so have friendships and marriages!

As leaders, we need to always properly choose the words we use. Our choice of words can affect our employees' behaviors, attitudes, and thoughts. Choosing correctly ensures that the effect we have on them is positive, motivating, and constructive. Once a word or a phrase is spoken, it cannot be taken back. If you don't get it right, the effects could be devastating and long lasting.

How Your Words Are Said

Your delivery matters! How you speak can change the meaning of what you are saying. Your tone can determine purpose, urgency, and emotion. Stressing certain words or phrases can help put an emphasis on important parts of your message. Volume levels can make you sound angry, unassertive, or somewhere in between. Your speech should always be positive and motivating, never projected in a tone that's angry, disappointed, stressed, or rushed. Never talk down to your employees; rather, talk to them directly, as valued team members.

Hone your delivery skills through ongoing practice. Always be evaluating yourself on how you communicate your messages to your employees. You may not realize how your speaking is being perceived. We are too well able to assess and immediately pick out the good, bad, and ugly in others, but not as much when it comes to assessing and identifying areas in which we need to improve. Give a friend or fellow leader the authority to assess and give honest feedback on how you speak to others. You probably have no idea how you sound. I know I didn't! When we don't know how we are managing or when we are managing badly, these are called blind spots. Often businesses have regular employees evaluate their bosses on a yearly basis.

I used to end all of my phone conversations with the phrase, "Have a pleasant day." I am not sure why or when I started doing so, but that was my tagline. I thought it was a friendly way to end a conversation. I truly wanted the person to whom I was speaking to have a pleasant day. My office staff all knew that this was my signature goodbye when I was ending a phone call. I started noticing that when they heard me say it, they would snicker, laugh, and snort. After seeing them amused for a long period of time by this simple statement, I decided to find out what was so funny.

I was surprised to find out that none of my employees thought my closing phrase was a kind way to end a call. They all said it sounded sarcastic! Although my words were wishing someone a pleasant day, my tone was just the opposite. They claimed that my tone made it sound like I was almost wishing the person to crash their car, suddenly develop appendicitis, or face other ill wishes.

I did not believe them, so they decided to record me engaging in my pleasant goodbye, without my knowledge. After gathering a couple of dozen recordings of me saying, "Have a pleasant day," my employees gathered at my office door and presented me their evidence. After I had listened to about seven or eight times of my saying my signature parting words, I shut the recorder off. My tone made a phrase that was supposed to be pleasant sound like a voodoo curse. I realized I was the Grim Reaper of telephone conversations! I made a change in my delivery immediately and began to assess how I said other things. I assigned my administrative assistant to be my "speech delivery" evaluator.

THOSE TECHNOLOGY MIXED MESSAGES

Messages sent via email, text, and other conduits are always being misinterpreted. Just like with speaking, written words have life too. They have their own tones, volume levels, and stressors. We have all received such messages, and we have all sent them. We find ourselves wondering if the sender is in a bad mood, agitated, or being rude on purpose. Usually upon inquiring as to what's behind the words we received, we find that the words we read were just that—words. These words were without any extra meanings or subtle messages. Most of us have been misunderstood as a result of the misinterpretation of the meaning of the words we sent to someone. That's not always the case, but usually.

Make sure you are not sending electronic communications filled with negative emotions. Everyone perceives things in their own unique way, so your email's overall tone should be positive. Start off with some personalized dialogue with the receiver. Ask them how they're doing, congratulate them on something they performed well, and say something encouraging. After the initial informal and friendly interaction, you can move on to your stated business. Don't construct electronic communications that are either too short or too long. Don't use all caps, emoticons, emojis, bolded

letters, or underlined words. Reread your email before sending it to be sure it's reader friendly and will be positively
received.

   Consider the following excerpt from an email
dialogue exchange when I was dealing with one of
my company's vendors about the completion of an
$80,000 truck we were having built and my thoughts
on the interaction:

   Me: Maxine, I hope your week is going well. I
know you mentioned our truck might be finished at
the end of next week. Can you check on the timeline
for me? Next week one of my employees is flying to an
airport about an hour from your location. If it works
out, I will fly him in on a one-way ticket on Friday
morning. He can pick up the truck and drive it back.
If it's not ready, I'll book him round trip.

   Maxine: HOW WILL HE GET TO OUR
FACTORY?

   Me: Maxine, we will figure that detail out if this
all works out. Can you let me know if the truck will
be completed on Friday so I can purchase his airline
ticket?

   Maxine: WHEN I GET BACK FROM LUNCH.

   Two days went by, and I had not received an email
back.

   Me: Hi, Maxine, I just want to keep the completion timeline on both of our radars. Did you find out
if the truck will be finished on Friday?

   Maxine: NO

Me: Maxine, just to be sure. No, it won't be done? Or you haven't been able to find out?

Maxine: NOT DONE.

The tone of Maxine's emails was made clear in several ways. She did not include a salutation in her emails, she used all capital letters, and her communications were short and terse. At one point she did not even email me back, and she was not cognizant of my mission to purchase a plane ticket. Her lack of customer service spanned everything from her not getting me the information I needed to the way she communicated with me in her written words.

Was she being rude, just busy, or not trained on how to communicate and provide customer service? Who knows? But her emailed words set the tone for a negative experience. I spoke to the owner about the poor customer service and how it had inconvenienced us. He told me that she was his sister-in-law, and because of that, he felt that he could not discipline her. He admitted that her personality was very rough and that he received a lot of complaints about her. We eventually stopped doing business with that company due to ongoing issues with customer service, as well as other deficiencies with their products.

BODY LANGUAGE

Our posture, facial expressions, gestures, and bodily movements speak an entire other language! Body language gives everyone around us another story beyond the words we are speaking. When I talk to someone, I often observe their body language more than I listen to their spoken words.

If there is an inconsistency between your spoken message and your body language, the true meaning of what you want to convey can be lessened, totally missed, or even discredited. That mixed messaging can not only distort what you are saying, but also possibly damage your team. It can cause them to doubt you and your sincerity. Your employees can end up feeling unmotivated and uninspired, which will hurt your profitability.

Leaders need to make sure they know how to use body language to add to their verbal messaging, rather than take away from it. Eye contact should always be steady, but not intimidating. Use your eyes to connect with your people. Make sure that your facial expressions are friendly and kind. Your body positioning should always be welcoming and approachable. Always make sure that your body movements are patient, agreeable, and cheerful. If you don't know how to positively utilize body language, learn how and practice using it correctly every day.

Interacting – Part 2

Make Small Talk Big

Making small talk is the way people "break the ice." It can be an excellent way for strangers to quickly build a rapport and get to know one another better. You can have small talk with your employees just make the small talk "big." The words, phrases, questions, and answers can be small, but the event of interaction should be "big." When you can use small talk effectively, it is a great way to develop and build deeper relationships.

There are several things you can do to accomplish big-small talk. Make it more than just "passing pleasantries," talking about the weather and current events. Sincerely be interested in the individuals who work for you—not your combined workforce, but each individual personally. Believe they have great things to contribute when you talk with them. Be genuinely interested in what they have to say, their thoughts, ideas, and life stories. Being interested should never end because there will always something new to learn about your employees. Their stories each have an infinite number of chapters that go deep and wide!

LISTENING MORE

Don't be a 50,000-watt blower! You are not conducting a seminar, nor are you preaching a revival meeting. You are interacting with important people who have meaningful things to share! Don't do all of the talking; do more listening. Notice I did not say hearing. Hearing what someone is saying is an ineffective method of engaging in a conversation. Listening is understanding what is being said to you. It is taking in the words being spoken, processing them, and then finding a way to relate to them. It's not hearing what you think is being said but receiving the message being communicated in its entirety—fully digesting every word, how those words are being said, and the body language that's accompanying the conversation.

I usually do not handle picking up materials for the employees that work for my contracting company. When I do, it's a rarity. My role in the company is not being a construction worker, although I know what needs to be done to complete the project. I also do not engage in the daily work, so I am not always sure if I am picking up the right thing when I do pitch in. Many of the employees that work for the big box home improvement stores aren't always sure about what the correct item is either.

One morning I got a call from one of my employees, asking if I could pick up a box of screws. He told me the length of the screw and what he was going to use it for. I arrived at the home improvement store and went straight to the screw department. I was having trouble finding the screws, so I looked for an employee to help me. I saw two staff members, a man and a woman. The man was helping someone else, so I asked the woman to help me. Her coworker heard my question and then turned his attention back to the customer he was helping. She immediately found me the right length I needed. I thanked her, and she walked away. I suddenly realized I had not asked her if the screws she had given me could be used for what we intended to use them for.

I could still see her walking away, but she was quite far from me. I didn't want to yell loudly to get her attention, so I asked the man that had been helping another customer if the screws I had would work for what we wanted to use them for. His response was, "She's good; she knows her stuff." I asked him my question again, and he said, "Just because she is a girl, that doesn't mean she doesn't know everything about construction."

I was a little annoyed and said, "It's not about man versus woman; it's about the screw usage. I asked her for a certain length, but I did not ask her if this screw type would work for our project."

He then rolled his eyes and stated, "This isn't a man's world anymore; she's at the top of her game when it comes to remodeling and construction." I gave up and ended up talking to a manager about the whole situation. It turned out that although I had the right length, I did indeed need a different style of screw.

> The second employee I was talking to was hearing me but not listening to my words. I repeated myself several times, but he only heard either what he thought he was hearing or what he wanted to hear.

When you are a leader that listens, you get the full story and can respond appropriately. Listening lessens the frequency of miscommunications and mistakes. Being a listener communicates to the speakers that you value them and what they are saying. It confirms the intended conversation and encourages further discussion.

ASK QUESTIONS

Effective communication also includes the exchange of questions between all parties involved in the conversation. Asking questions can elicit responses that not only provide information, but also spark ideas and solutions that haven't been thought of yet. Questions convey that all parties involved in the conversation are valued. Their input is being sought because it is highly regarded. If you formulate your questions with sincere curiosity, you never run out of things to ask.

Ask questions that elicit not simply yes or no answers, but responses that require some creative thinking. The feedback you receive will consist of well-thought-out and meaningful answers. When your employees see that they are providing beneficial contributions, they will see themselves as valuable members of the team. This will build their confidence and cause them to want to share more ideas. The increase in their confidence will transform them into not only a better employee, but also a better person.

ASK CHALLENGING QUESTIONS

Your questions should positively challenge your people. Questions should be constructed to defy traditional thinking, existing assumptions, and the way things have always been done. Such questions should motivate your team members to become divergent thinkers and help them to birth novel ideas and solutions, thus promoting an organization filled with people who are not problem reactors or avoiders, but proactive problem solvers. This environment will lessen your being needed to figure out how to fix things, allowing you to do what you are supposed to do: lead, mentor, and motivate your employees to greater levels of performance and productivity.

SUMMARIZE

Validate the conversations you have by summarizing what was discussed. This will ensure that everyone participating in the conversation shares a general understanding of what was said. This practice fosters team unity about the objectives being set forth and establishes a concerted effort to reach those goals. The result will be a goal-oriented team working integrally with one another to achieve results that are beneficial to the entire organization.

DON'T HIDE

Be a leader who is always there for his employees. Some managers hunker down in their office like it is a doomsday bunker, never showing their face. Others claim to have the proverbial open door, where every employee always has access to them. Most rarely live up to that claim! These scenarios lead to employees' feeling undervalued, neglected, unimportant, and lacking needed leadership.

Make sure you really do have an open-door policy. Take your office door off its hinges if you must! And don't wait for your employees to come to you. Go to them. Get out of your office and get in the trenches with your people. Interact, collaborate, and connect with them as often as you can. Your staff will see you more as a team member than as the "dreaded boss" most managers are viewed as. Your involvement will endear them to you and cause them to have a greater respect for you. When they see you becoming more involved, they will get jump in and become more involved themselves.

Don't Gossip About Others

Never speak negatively about anyone in your organization. Your team should never know if you have negative opinions about someone. If you can't get along with someone or if you have disagreements with them, your staff should be clueless. If you are discussing anyone, specifically a person you do not mesh with, only say positive things. You won't be lying because everyone has positives. Even when you are sure they don't, examine them at length with unfiltered lenses. You'll find an extensive list of good things in time! Make those discovered positives your talking points when discussing that person you disagree with.

When discussing coworkers, never use positive-negative sentences such as, "Bill is a hard worker; it's too bad he..." or

---

"God love her, she does her best, but..." or my favorite, "If you can look past...." If you are going to use positive-negative sentences, you might as well drop the positives and just use negatives.

SPEAKING WITHOUT WORDS

Don't make the mistake of speaking positively about a person about whom you feel negatively, thus negating the good nonverbally. Make sure your facial expressions and bodily gestures are also positives. When a coworker's name is mentioned and you instantly grimace, you won't be able to dress things up with a positive phrase. When someone is talking about one of your team members and you roll your eyes or sigh loudly, there is no way to overcome the impression you have given.

I have never forgotten my sixth-grade teacher, whom I will call Mrs. Bartley. Mrs. Bartley was known for being the strictest teacher at the school. She was also famous for being downright mean. She wasn't shy about giving an angry tongue-lashing to both students and teachers alike. She rarely praised anyone, unless you were her "pet" student. If you were on her favorite's list, she would lather on the love and praise. If you weren't, you knew you wouldn't receive any accolades, and you were probably going to hear how worthless you were.

She was so transparent about her feelings that she didn't have to say a word for you to know how she felt. She often made statements about one of her students, paired with obvious body language. When she did this, there was no confusion about the message she was dispensing. It was totally clear!

Mrs. Bartley scheduled a talent show where every student had to perform for our class. The students were going to judge each act based on applause. Several elimination rounds were to be held until only the top two students were left. The two finalists then had to perform against one another to determine who the final winner would be.

There were singers, dancers, a ventriloquist, an accordion player, a trombone player, and a variety of other acts. A friend of mine named Bill did some tricks with his yo-yo, and another girl, Michelle, played the piano. At that stage of my life, I saw myself as some sort of Harry Houdini and decided to perform as a magician. Mrs. Bartley's fair-haired favorite student, Paul, was going to recite some poetry he had written.

The combination of my being shy and nervous and Mrs. Bartley's rolling her eyes and announcing to the class that we all knew magic wasn't real, I was voted out quite early. My friend Bill did some amazing yo-yo tricks, but Mrs. Bartley harpooned him from the running before he even began to perform. When he walked up in front of the class, she began to wrinkle her nose and proceeded to pinch it shut. She cruelly declared, "Someone smells like urine." She emphasized the word urine and at the same time quickly turned her head and looked at Bill.

She then followed up with, "They must wet the bed every night and not take a bath before school. They reek of pee every day." The class groaned, and many kids booed and yelled, "Gross." Bill and I were very close friends, and we had both had sleepovers at each other's house many times. I never knew him to wet the bed, nor did he ever smell like pee.

In the end, Paul and Michelle were the remaining acts. Mrs. Bartley had them perform one last time and then had them stand on either side of her so the students could applaud for the best act. Michelle was a brilliant pianist, while Paul was a horrible poet. The class resoundingly voted for Michelle as the winner with thunderous applause, and Paul barely got any claps.

Mrs. Bartley was clearly angry that Paul was not the winner. She decided to have another round of applause to try to garner more votes for Paul. On the second vote, she downplayed Michelle's performance, quickly asked for applause, and almost before anyone could begin clapping, she ordered everyone to quiet down. The sound of the clapping was much less than in the first round of judging, where Michelle had been the clear winner.

When it came time for the class to judge Paul, she spent several minutes shamelessly praising him. Then before she asked the class to applaud, she spent some more time firing the students up by waving her arms in the air like a cheerleader and getting them to loudly practice their applauding. Once the excitement in the room had been stirred up and was nearly out of control, she called for Paul's voting to begin. There was a deafening outpour of hand clapping and cheering for Paul, declaring him the talent contest winner.

Michelle was crushed, and I think even scarred for life, by this event and some other despicable things Mrs. Bartley did to her that school year. Mrs. Bartley's facial expressions, gestures, and other covert activities had swayed the class to vote for Paul. We all knew Michelle was the true winner and that Mrs. Bartley had corrupted the voting process. But none of us challenged Mrs. Bartley, and we never talked about it after that.

Several decades later Mrs. Bartley was forced to retire early for insulting and bullying certain students. She picked the wrong students to treat poorly, and word got out about it through social media. When I was in her class, we did not have a conduit to spread the word throughout the community when we were mistreated. I have discussed Mrs. Bartley's fate with several former students of hers. We all felt vindicated and happy to see her removed from teaching. Many said that her cruelty had affected them negatively in ways that lasted for years.

Don't be a leader that sways "votes" on employees by tainting your team's mind with body language and negativity. Such behavior will hurt office relationships, team cohesiveness, employee productivity, and company profits. The entire company suffers when you sow the seeds of negativity through gossip and talking behind people's backs.

Everyone knows that if you are willing to talk about one employee to another employee, you will do the same thing to them. Negativity and gossip will make you look bad and cause your staff not to trust you. They will put up walls and feel they must be guarded around you. No one will feel comfortable being open with you, so they will never be transparent. Your leadership will become handicapped or even useless.

BE YOURSELF

Be you! Interacting with people is always easier when you are not putting on an act or hiding something. There's no need to write a humorous script that entertains an audience. Feeling the pressure to engage in perfect conversations is not required. Have real, unscripted conversations that have a sincere personal touch. Just relax. Let your true personality speak through you and enjoy interacting with your people. You will absolutely love the relationships and team building that will occur, transforming your organization into something great.

The A.C.E. in the
Ace of Hearts

The Check Off List

Most leadership training has a bullet-point list of qualities that every great leader must possess. If you check off all the right boxes, you are granted "Great Leader Status!" This list often includes the following:

- Be confident
- Be inspiring
- Be passionate
- Be an effective communicator
- Be a good decision maker
- And the list goes on

These qualities, among others, are very important for leaders to possess if they want to be great leaders. However, the *Ace of Heart* leader's list of just three points.

The A in the *Ace of Hearts*: Accept

At my house, we absolutely love dogs. We don't love the mud they track into the house, the hair they shed on the carpet, the occasional mess they make, nor the penchant for chewing to pieces our belongings; these negative characteristics don't make them loveable. What makes our dogs loveable is how they react when they see us come through the front door. It's their running to us with excitement, their furiously wagging tails, and the wet kisses they greet us with.

Our dogs are always lovingly happy to see us, no matter what. Even if I have had a bad day and completely ignore them, act frustrated with them, or push them away, they still pour on the love: a love bestowed regardless of my actions. Dogs tend to accept and love their families right where they are.

I Can't Change Anyone

I realized years ago I'm unable to truly change every employee. An employee's desire to change and the act of change must come from within. It's totally up to the employee and no one else. *Ace of Hearts* leaders who accept their employees right where they are possess one of the three keys needed to grant life-changing power, a power that comes not from trying to change people, but rather from guiding them to want to make changes on their own. This power is used to effortlessly facilitate changes in behavior because someone wants to change, not because you are forcing them to.

You do not want the temporary changes most leaders see when they resort to twisting their employees' arms behind their backs in an attempt to "fix" them—the type of change that vanishes when management is not nearby micromanaging their every move. Your desire is to facilitate change that responds to love, not fear. Real, lasting change

———

in your employees comes when they realize you love and accept them unconditionally.

Accept and celebrate the fact that many individuals are different than you. Understand that they have the right to be themselves, entitled to independent beliefs, ideas, feelings, and opinions. Show them they can be different from you and their coworkers without fear of being judged or rejected.

An *Ace of Hearts* leader must be the example when it comes to the "A" in the *Ace of Hearts*. To start, you must put your full attention on yourself: truly embracing who you are as a person, all the while striving to identify your own character and personality traits that need improvement. With this knowledge, you can begin making the effort to strengthen the areas in your life that are lacking. Be the role model of "Accept"" to everyone on your staff!

Once you learn to accept yourself, an amazing thing happens. You can begin to accept others from a vantage point of nonjudgment. You will begin to see everyone else through an uncomplicated lens, seeing more of their good and less of their bad. Doing so comes with great benefits to each individual employee, the team, and the overall company. It brings the group closer and builds trust among peers. It allows individuals to be themselves without fear of rejection or judgment. When the pressure is off, people actually perform at a much higher level.

Does this mean a leader must accept poor work performance? Absolutely not. It means you accept an individual right where they are as a person: their quirks, their hurts, their annoyances, and any other negative. Everyone has negatives, and you should be okay with those negatives, even if

———

you don't approve of some of them. You'll begin to understand how differences are opportunities, rather than obstacles.

Real change, when it comes to an employee's performance, can and will occur in time. This happens when you build deeper relationships with your staff. Getting them to understand that you are interested in helping them become better in every area of their lives is the key—not for you, not for the company, but for them! From there you move on to the next step, which is challenging them to do better. Better in every area of their life! Once the bond is developed and trust has been established, you can begin the next step of challenging them to grow and improve themselves. Don't ever stop accepting, loving, and building relationships with your people.

The C in the *Ace of Hearts*: **Challenge**

An *Ace of Hearts* leader needs to be a good role model when it comes to the "C" in the *Ace of Hearts*. To do so, you must transparently push yourself to grow. Step out of your comfort zone, drive yourself out of complacency, and take on new challenges. Be willing to admit your mistakes, accept input, and adjust your direction when needed. Be confident, but humble. Show your willingness to undertake the challenges that come with your position. Be the example of "Challenge" to everyone on your team!

Then motivate your employees to step out of their safe place—not to be stagnant at work or in their personal lives, but to always make progress towards something better. When leaders encounter a challenge, they should have a desire to meet it head on and overcome it. When they do, they feel a sense of accomplishment. Overcoming challenges builds employee confidence.

Regularly assign challenging, but achievable tasks to your employees, tasks that force them into unchartered waters. Doing so lets the employees know how much confidence you have in their abilities. However, make sure you do not designate an employee to handle an assignment at which they will fail. Doing so will hobble their confidence and possibly hinder their ability to perform their job effectively. The more success they achieve, the more they will experience positive growth!

They won't always succeed at their challenges. When they do fail, use the failure as a positive teaching moment. Begin the teaching moment by being gentle, forgiving, and supportive. Point out the many successes found within their failure. Add up all the points they scored, show them how close they were to a win and how much they actually accomplished. Remind them that the effort alone, which they poured into the task you assigned them, was a personal win for them.

Share some of your biggest failures with them and excitedly share what knowledge you garnered as a result of those failures. Let them know how you learned from failing and how it helped you later in your life. Welcome questions as to what they could have done differently and what the outcome might have been if they had made different choices. Make them come up with viable solutions that would have worked better. Develop the "problem solver" within them that they are not confident enough to see. Never give up but stay on mission to challenge your employees to experience positive growth daily.

Lastly, challenge your employees to become better

citizens, to be active in their community, and to consider volunteering for causes they feel compelled to support. Encourage them to be kind, compassionate, and respectful to their neighbors, taking responsibility for their actions and governing themselves accordingly.

THE E IN THE *ACE OF HEARTS*: **ENCOURAGE**

An *Ace of Hearts* leader must set the bar high when it comes to the "E" in the *Ace of Hearts*. You must always be an encouragement to yourself. This is achieved by identifying your strengths, capitalizing on them, and continuing to work on your deficiencies. Always be optimistic about yourself and your abilities. Be confident that you and your team can overcome any challenge. Assure yourself that you and your team are an unstoppable and unshakable force.

Pass on to your team members the confidence you convey to yourself. Help them self-recognize their strengths and how to effectively utilize them. Prompt them to search out and discover them on their own. Self-discovery builds confidence, drives people to use their strengths to achieve success, and encourages them to grow. Motivate them to identify and accept their deficiencies. Lead them to work on their weaknesses so they can have a greater career and a better life.

Invite your employees to become problem solvers by allowing them to share their input and make decisions and by delegating greater responsibilities to them. Assure them you trust them and actually mean it! Make them feel valuable and worthy of a lifelong career with your organization. Assist them in planning their future with your company and help them plan out their life.

Do life with your employees! Don't be an encouragement just at the workplace, but in every area of their lives. Inspire and motivate them, whether they are struggling at the bottom of one of life's valleys or happily dancing on a mountaintop. Encouragement always leads upward, no matter where they are in life!

Promote an *Ace of Hearts* Culture

Always cultivate an *Ace of Hearts* environment in your organization. If you are passionate and excited about the company's *Ace of Hearts* goals, your team members will realize your vision as well. As employees continue to catch the vision, it will quickly spread throughout the company. Encourage your employees to become *Ace of Hearts* ambassadors at work, at home, and in the community.

Never Give Up

I believe most people desire to have deep, intimate relationships, where they are valued, loved, and cared for without judgment or strings attached. They want one person in their life they can count on—the friend they can call at 3:00 a.m. during a blizzard who will actually answer the phone! This friend would answer with concern and a willingness to head out into the cold darkness for their friend. Undeterred by white-out conditions, drifting, and icy roads, this friend would quickly arrive to rescue them from danger. People may not always express the desire to have such a friend, and sometimes they deliberately suppress it. They may hide it, act like it doesn't exist, and even deny it, but the desire is there.

A true *Ace of Hearts* leader doesn't have to be just an

employer. The *Ace of Hearts* leader can be one employee building a relationship with another employee. They "do life" together, both inside and outside of the workplace. Your position in the company guarantees you'll be involved in your employees' work lives. You will "do life" together at work, but not every employee will allow you to become involved in their personal life, and that's alright. It's their decision whether or not to be mentored or to have a relationship with other employees, supervisors, or business owners. As your employees get to know and experience an *Ace of Hearts* relationship with you, they may change their mind about such a relationship. The *Ace of Hearts* experience can change the toughest people, so never give up.

Gary Horvath worked for almost ten years as a correctional officer at a maximum-security prison before being hired as a police officer. He had dreamed of being a police officer since he was a child. He had been thrilled to quit his job at the prison and headed off to attend the police academy. He couldn't wait to graduate from the police academy so he could start working the streets. Upon graduation, he was assigned to work with a training officer, Sergeant James Kelly, for three months.

During his tenure with the department of corrections, Gary had witnessed violence almost daily. Inmates argued with, cursed at, and threatened the correctional staff and other inmates. Correctional officers faced the possibility of having bodily waste thrown on them, being punched, kicked, or assaulted with deadly weapons—assaults that could easily result in permanent injury or even death.

Inmates were continually lying and trying to con the correctional staff. This background had caused Gary to become mistrustful of everyone around him, causing others to wonder if he was suffering from paranoia. His mistrust, combined with the level of stress he experienced at work, eventually affected his mental and physical health. The strain affected his personal relationships, specifically his marriage. After a rocky five years, his wife divorced him, not wanting to see him at all but allowing him to spend time with his children. Gary felt betrayed, causing him to become even more suspicious of people with whom he interacted. He began limiting his communications and interactions with people, placing his focus on his job, trying to be hired by a police department, and spending time with his children.

On his first official night of being a police officer, Gary met up with his training officer, James Kelly. James introduced himself and said, "Hey, buddy, I'm James Kelly, but you can call me Jim. Well, all the cops here call me Jimbo, and since we are going to spend three months together, you can call me Jimbo too."

Gary replied, "Nice to meet you Sergeant Kelly." Gary jumped into the passenger seat to ride so Jim could start training him. Several times Jim reminded him it was alright to call him Jim or Jimbo. Gary responded, "Let's keep it professional. At the prison we addressed each other by rank and last name or by last name only. I'd rather address you as Sergeant Kelly or just Kelly."

Throughout the next three months, Sergeant Kelly tried to get know his trainee better. He and some of the other officers routinely asked Gary to hang out with them after work or get together on their days off. Gary always refused and kept everyone completely shut out of his personal life.

After his training, Gary was permanently assigned to Sergeant Kelly's crew. They ended up sharing the same days off and worked most of the same days together. They spent a lot of time together responding to calls, having coffee or a meal together, and parking next to each other to talk. Sergeant Kelly shared his faith with Gary, often talking about his family and telling other personal stories. Gary jokingly made fun of him for going to church. When Jim brought up his wife and kids, Gary would gruffly say he was never going to get married again. Jim accepted Gary's personal issues and surly demeanor. Jim knew Gary had experienced lots of hurts in his past, so Jim chose to be a loving coworker and friend.

Sometimes Sergeant Kelly would have to take the lead with Gary, documenting mistakes he had made. When he counseled Gary, he always did it with love. Most of the time, Jim would begin by commenting on the areas where Gary was doing a wonderful job. He never stayed focused very long on Gary's negative behavior. He would address what had been done improperly, suggest where Gary could improve himself, and move on. Once the correction was administered, it was not brought up again. Sergeant Kelly continually challenged and encouraged Gary to become a better police officer and a better human being. He never gave up or stopped being Gary's *Ace of Hearts* leader.

Two years later, Gary experienced a tragedy in his life. His dad was killed while out riding his motorcycle. The first person Gary called was Sergeant Kelly. Sergeant Kelly rushed over to Gary's house to console him and knocked on his door. When Gary yanked the door open, he burst into tears and cried out, "Jimbo, help me. My dad's gone." The two of them embraced as Gary began to weep uncontrollably. In over two years of working together, Gary had never called Sergeant James Kelly "Jimbo." At that moment, the ice wasn't just broken; it was completely melted.

Jimbo helped Gary make arrangements for his dad's funeral. He took a week's worth of vacation time so he could be there for Gary during his time of grief. Their relationship grew stronger in the months following the funeral. The two of them began to spend time together on their off time. Jimbo spent many hours teaching Gary. He taught him how to put his past hurts behind him and be more positive. Little by little, Gary began to share his life story with Jimbo, which allowed the two of them to bond more closely. Knowing Gary's past adversities allowed Jimbo to counsel more effectively.

Gary got to know Jimbo's wife and children and carefully watched the family interact. He was amazed at how happy they were and how much they loved each other. He noticed how they enjoyed life's simple things: a sunset, the garden they had planted together, or going out for ice cream. They never exchanged harsh words or raised their voices at one another. The conversations were always worded sweetly, and they enjoyed being together. Gary's marriage had never come close to what he witnessed. He and his wife had never enjoyed spending time together. When they did, they ended up arguing.

Gary's life began to evolve in a better direction. He began attending Jimbo's church and became involved in some outreach projects in his community. One day Gary was passing out donated backpacks and school supplies to children of single moms. One of those single moms, Regina, caught his eye. They began to date, fell in love, and eventually married. Jimbo was proud to be the best man at the wedding. Gary's new family was just the opposite of his first marriage. Like Jimbo, he began to appreciate the little things he experienced with his new family. He and his wife actually enjoyed spending time together and were often teased by their friends for being too lovey-dovey.

Gary rose through the ranks of the police department and received many commendations for his actions. He is known for selflessly serving the citizens who reside in his city. He and his wife spend their time together being *Ace of Hearts* leaders, helping hurting and needy people improve their lives.

Four of My Personal *Ace of Hearts* Leaders

M Y LIFE HAS been filled with an abundance of *Ace of Hearts* leaders. Sometimes it was a CEO that filled that role, but more often, it was everyday people that I encountered on my life's journey. The *Ace of Hearts* leader role they filled in my life was secondary to their primary role. Some were educators, small business owners, friends, family members, and even a stranger. Each one uniquely contributed to one or more areas of my life. This chapter will introduce you to four of my personal *Ace of Hearts* leaders and what they did to positively impact my life. Further examples can be found in my online *Ace of Hearts* Leadership course, offered through my company website: www.traininglion.com.

Edmund Crabb

Some *Ace of Hearts* leaders impact your life, even when they think their influence isn't having any affect. I was an extremely shy, chubby, and socially out-of-step 13-year-old when I attended middle school. I vividly remember walking into my seventh-grade science class on the first day of the school year. There were lab tables with microscopes, beakers, Bunsen burners, and test tubes. The room had an unusual smell I'd never experienced before. I am not sure if it was a mixture of formaldehyde and other science class chemicals, but I never forgot it. If I am in the science department of a school or college campus, that odor is always present.

I found my seat, and just as the bell rang, my new science teacher walked in. He was young, wore glasses, and was dressed in a white lab coat. I was slightly intimidated because the lab coat made him look like a doctor. He introduced himself to the class. "My name is Mr. Crabb. I am going to be your science teacher this year." That day began the best year of all the years I attended school.

Mr. Crabb brought science alive! He made every minute of that one-hour class fun and interesting. When a teacher inspires you to listen to their lectures and then you rush home and study the material, getting a good grade is almost effortless.

But there was more. Mr. Crabb wasn't just interested in our learning science. He was sincerely interested in his students. He took time to get know us not just as students, but as human beings. He never brushed us off or acted bothered to interact with us. He also was willing to stay late after school so a couple of other students and I could do extra science activities. I stayed after school every time he was there. We did many interesting experiments, and I was able to work on a project about pacemakers for the science fair. I earned a second-place award!

During the first couple of months of the school year, I bought my very own white lab jacket, a dissection pan, a microscope, and a chemistry set. I set up my own lab in a spare room in my basement. For my Christmas present wish list, I requested test tubes, beakers, a graduated cylinder, and a subscription to Scientific American magazine. That year I spent many evenings and Saturdays in my makeshift lab believing I was a scientist.

Towards the end of the school year, I was looking forward to the next year's science class. I found out I might have a different teacher, so I stopped by the science office to ask Mr. Crabb if that were true. I told him what I had heard and asked if it was possible to have him as my teacher in eighth grade. I remember his looking at me sadly when he said, "Brad, I won't be here next year. The money I am getting paid isn't enough to take care of my family. After school lets out, I'm starting a job as a chemist at a local oil refinery."

I was crushed, but I did not want him to know it. I told him, "That's great! I'm happy for you." I walked out of the science office, and as soon as I was out of earshot, I began to cry. I ran down the hall to the parking lot. I remember wondering if I would ever have another teacher that cared about me as much as Mr. Crabb did—a teacher whom I loved. As the years went by, my question was answered. I never experienced a teacher like him again.

I had not seen Mr. Crabb for almost 36 years. A few years ago, we reconnected on social media and were able to have a meal together. He was retired and almost 70 years old. Since then, we have stayed in touch and communicate often. I asked him what caused him to be the type of teacher he was, what I would call an *Ace of Hearts* leader.

He responded, "When I started teaching, I thought my passion was for teaching science, but it did not take me long to see what my true passion was. It was for the kids in that age group. Nothing inside of me stirred the passion; it was the students. I felt like each one was my own child, and I tried, sometimes desperately, to give them the tools they would need for school and for life. I always felt I failed more than I succeeded at that. It was a challenge saying good-bye at the end of the year and getting ready for a new batch of students the following school year. I am very humbled by the fact that I apparently affected you as much as I did. It was an easy connection to make with you. Your enthusiasm and attitude made it easy to reach out and relate. The jocks and popular kids did not always respond the same way or seem to need the attention like some of the others in the class. I found it rewarding when I could brighten their lives a little, help pull them out of their shell, and make them feel like they had value.

"I hope this helps a little, but the truth is that if I could explain how teachers and students connect, I would bottle the formula and give it away free to every school in the nation. The truth of it! It is the work and guidance from God that connects the kids in the classroom with the teachers they need and the other way around. I do not feel I was an exceptional teacher and almost never felt like I was doing enough. Perhaps it is being sincere and not a fake that makes a difference."

Bill Colfax

I was 17 years old. I had just graduated from high school and rented my first apartment on Chicago's Northside. That same apartment presently rents for nearly $3000 a month, but back then I was only paying $350! I was working the evening shift as a stocker at a local grocery store, making only $3.35 an hour. My monthly income barely paid my rent and utilities. I knew I needed to get a second full-time job if I wanted to eat and have a little bit of spending money.

A few days after I moved in, I woke up at 5am to buy a newspaper. I wanted to get an early start perusing the help wanted ads to find that second job. As I walked out of my apartment building, I saw a gray-haired man sweeping the sidewalk in front of a business. He looked at me with a big smile and said, "Good morning, kid. Why are you up so early and where are you off to?"

I replied, "I always get up early. I'm headed out to find a job."

He laughed and said, "Look no further! My name's Bill Colfax, and I'm about to become your new boss!"

Bill offered me a position as a citywide delivery driver, taking his products to customers that ordered them. He asked if I'd quit the grocery store to work for him 12 hours a day, Monday through Saturday. He offered me a salary of $350 a week, which was $1400 a month.

I immediately pondered the positives of his offer. Although my pay would only average out to $4.86 an hour, I wouldn't have to travel back and forth to two different jobs twice a day. I would only be one minute away from work, so there wouldn't be a long commute. He then offered to buy me breakfast every morning if I'd be ready for him to pick me up at 5 a.m. I stuck out my hand and asked, "When can I start?"

He shook my hand and answered, "In two weeks. I will only hire you if you give the grocery store two weeks' notice that you're quitting, and you must work those two weeks."

Two weeks later I began spending my days delivering his products to businesses around the city. I learned the Chicago streets quite well, but my real education was the time spent with Bill, specifically our time together at breakfast and throughout the day when there weren't any deliveries.

I'll never forget Bill, the first *Ace of Hearts* leader that mentored me as an adult man. He was my first boss at what I considered to be a real job. If it were not for him, I believe I would never have experienced all of the successes that I've had in life. Without Bill, I might never have learned how to accept, learn from, and move on from adversity. I truly feel that Bill loved me and had a sincere desire to mentor me with wisdom that would better my life. He took the time to get to know me, listen to me, and answer my questions. He never once told me he was too busy to talk or spend time with me.

Bill opened unfiltered windows into many of his life's experiences. He shared not only his personal and business successes, but also his failures. From that transparency, I began to gather a great deal of wisdom, knowledge, and information. Bill taught me about business, personal relationships, dating, love, finances, and a plethora of other things. He schooled me in problem solving and leadership skills, which I utilize almost daily. I am not sure if Bill ever realized he was molding me into something better, but he was.

Just knowing that Bill was willing to invest in my life made me feel worthy and increased my confidence. Although it was one of the lowest paying jobs I have ever had, it was one of the best jobs I have ever had. I didn't have a fancy title or position. I was just a delivery boy, but Bill always made me feel valued. This is the positive influence a single *Ace of Hearts* leader can have on a life.

A few years ago, I visited Bill at his home. He was days away from departing this earth. His health was failing fast, and dementia had set in. Although he had forgotten my name, he perfectly remembered and spoke of many wonderful memories we had shared together. We talked, laughed, and cried that day, and my emotions ran wild. A week later his wife called me to let me know of his passing. I hope that one day when I breathe my last breath, I will do so knowing that I was the best *Ace of Hearts* leader I could ever be.

MARIA PIZANO

Some *Ace of Hearts* leaders share knowledge with you that change your financial situation. I had dreamed about being a real estate investor since I was a teenager. At that young age, I would look through the local newspaper's real estate ads, trying to figure out how I could one day own rental properties and flip houses. After I graduated from high school, I gave up on that dream because I felt I'd never have enough money to invest in real estate.

I became friends with a woman named Maria Pizano. When I first met her, I was financially struggling to get by. One day over lunch, I shared my real estate investing dream with her. Maria interjected, "Buy some rental properties, wholesale a couple of properties a month, and flip a few houses a year. With the money you'll make, you'll stop working overtime, and you'll quit your second job. You might even quit your full-time job!"

I laughed and said, "I don't have any money to invest in real estate."

She responded, "Brad, you don't always need money to invest in real estate. I own several houses that I acquired while I was broke!" We had just become friends, so I never knew she was a real estate investor. She shared with me how she became a real estate investor while living paycheck to paycheck and how she had been able to buy properties with little or no money down by utilizing creative financing techniques.

She told me, "Brad, you could do it too. I can teach you how."

"Maria," I interrupted, "aside from the money constraints, I don't want to be fixing plugged toilets and leaky pipes in the middle of the night. Besides that, I'm not a plumber. I don't know how to do that stuff."

Maria replied, "I already explained that you don't need any money. People always fearfully say something about plumbing when I talk about real estate investing. It's a myth! Plumbers don't come out in the middle of the night to make repairs. You must wait for them to come out during business hours. Your tenants would have to do the same."

She convinced me to chase my dream and promised to help me realize that dream. After a few months of mentoring and looking at a lot of houses, I bought my first property without any money. I immediately got an equity line against that house and bought a second "no money down home." I continued to accumulate properties by utilizing the techniques Maria taught me. When I first met Maria, I had no idea she would be an *Ace of Hearts* leader who shared knowledge with me that would change my financial situation.

PUNNAWIT SHRADER

Some *Ace of Hearts* leaders make you see the world differently than you ever did before. When I was dating my wife, Punnawit, I realized she was different than anyone I had ever known. She always takes a sincere interest in everything she does and everyone she meets. She views everything around her as worthy of her full attention. I almost think the flowers and plants in her garden feel valued by the way she cares for them. Is it possible that the hummingbirds, butterflies, rabbits, and other animals that live on our property feel her excitement as she admires, smiles, and comments on their beauty? My wife has taught me to take the time to be genuinely interested in the things around me, to enjoy and admire everyone and everything that crosses my path.

She sees both chance and planned encounters with people as important events. Whether it's a brief encounter with a stranger or a lifelong relationship, she devotes herself to making each interaction memorable and special. Her actions inspire me to be an *Ace of Hearts* leader, one who regards every interaction as important and unforgettable and who sees each encounter as an opportunity to take a sincere interest in another person's life.

Punnawit always sees the good in people and experiences. Somehow the negatives of those same people or events seem to escape her senses. She doesn't just overlook the imperfections of others; she never picks up on them. If I point out a negative, she says, "We all have bad parts about us. Thankfully everyone has such an abundance of good in them, that the bad doesn't poison all of the positives." This has taught me to focus on the good. Don't search for the bad. Accept others unconditionally.

Gratitude is one of Punnawit's qualities that amazes me the most. I remember the first time I noticed it. It was over 100 degrees when she saw some workers hanging on to the back of a garbage truck. She watched them intently as they were working hard to empty garbage cans into the truck in the extreme heat. She looked at me and said, "I really appreciate them and what they are doing so much. It's so hot. The garbage must smell horrible, and they're still working very hard. They are doing a job that many people would think they are too good to do. I am so thankful for them being willing to serve us and the community in the humble way they do." Take note. She noticed them, thought about the job they were doing, and expressed gratitude for their being willing to do so. I didn't even see them, let alone think about them or their difficult job in barely tolerable conditions.

My wife expresses appreciation for everything, whether big or small. I could take her to Disney World for a vacation or Dairy Queen for a Blizzard, and she would be equally thankful. She is grateful for the cook at the restaurant that prepares our meals and the server that brings us the food.

She appreciates the restaurant greeter and the people that bus the tables. She values police officers, firefighters, and EMTs. She is thankful for our military and the sacrifices they make to protect us. She is especially grateful for the freedoms and opportunities America presents to everyone.

Through constant examples of gratitude displayed by her actions and her words, she has taught me to be grateful for everything, to be quick to let others know I appreciate them and what they have done, and to never take anything for granted because somebody has sacrificed or worked hard for whatever it may be. It is a great honor to be married to and "do life" with Punnawit as one of my Personal *Ace of Hearts* leaders.

ACE OF HEARTS
HIRING

HIRING STRATEGIES WHICH ADVANCE AN *ACE OF HEARTS* PHILOSOPHY

Candidates going through the application process simultaneously receive company micro-training. Their classroom is the interview room, and their trainer is the interviewer. Every interaction that occurs is educating them about the organization, its operations and culture. Phone calls, emails, phone interviews and in-person interviews are just a few of the topics covered. The entire hiring process should be organized and professional. Phone and email communications should never go unanswered. Communications with applicants need to be welcoming, kind, and courteous. Scheduled interviews should be conducted punctually, never having the candidate wait for more than a few minutes. It's frowned upon if an applicant is late for an interview; it usually eliminates them from the hiring process. The interviewer should be held to the same standard. Positive and negative experiences instruct jobseekers on what to expect if they are selected for employment.

SAY GOODBYE TO TRADITIONAL METHODS

Your employees are the key to your organization's success. Recruiting people who will be an acceptable match for the *Ace of Hearts* company you're striving to create won't always be accomplished via traditional hiring practices. Recruiting the most qualified applicants won't necessarily help you achieve that goal. Hiring the job-hunter with the right degree or a stack of certificates may not be the best choice for the *Ace of Hearts* culture you desire. A stellar resume you're excitingly reading might not yield the results you crave desire. All the "rights" that traditional employee selection dictates may produce a lot of wrongs for your organization—wrongs that could hobble what you are trying to accomplish.

SOURCING PROSPECTS

If you are truly an *Ace of Hearts* company, sourcing won't be your biggest problem. Your biggest problem will be the flood of jobseekers who will be trying to get you to employ them! When the word gets out how your company and its leadership is different than the other businesses in your area, you will be swamped with job applicants. I've personally experienced this with my own companies. My competitors' employees would constantly call or drop by my office asking for a job. Friends, family members, neighbors, and strangers were always sending in resumes. When asked why, they would reply something like this, "Everyone around town knows this is 'the place' to work. It's well known you care about your people."

At the time this chapter is being written, one man is

moving from California to just outside of Chicago to work for one of my companies. He resigned a posh, six-figure job to work for me. He sold his house and most of his belongings and is driving across the country with his family in about three weeks to relocate here. His making the choice to relocate halfway across the country to work for me is not only humbling but also honoring as well! I am not sure I would make the same move. I am providing him free housing and utilities for the first year so he can get settled in. That timeline is flexible and could be extended if he hasn't found a suitable home in the first year. He is going to be compensated well, receive performance bonuses, insurance, an expense account, profit sharing, and after some longevity, stock options.

You might be wondering what position he is taking to garner such an employment package, thinking to yourself, "This must not be an entry level position." You're correct. It is not an entry level position. It's an executive team leadership role. Your response to those details might be, "I knew it! You've got to treat your top people right, but none of that would be offered to someone who's just a regular employee."

Not so fast! Seven weeks ago, I hired a skilled construction worker named Peter, who resided in another state. He's also receiving free housing for the first year with his employment offer. He'll also be paid performance bonuses, insurance, profit sharing, and eventually receive stock options. He isn't receiving an expense account, because it isn't something his role requires. Instead, each year he'll be receiving seven pairs of shorts, seven pairs of pants, and seven company shirts. He's also going to be issued a fall/spring jacket and a battery-powered winter jacket, which heats up for working in extremely cold weather conditions.

Presently, your company may not be able to afford to compensate employees and provide them with a benefits package like that. You can work towards being able to do so as your company's profitability increases. You currently may only be able to offer bonuses, profit sharing, paid vacations, and stock options. "We can't even do that right now!" you may respond with sadness. I've been there too, but there are other *Ace of Hearts* acts you can perform! These actions don't cost a lot of money but can make your employees feel valued and appreciated—even if they are just small gestures of gratitude.

Over the years, I have had to do many inexpensive *Ace of Hearts* acts of appreciation for my people, especially when my company was a startup and I was struggling to grow it. Sometimes it was tough to meet my weekly payroll, and other times I could not even afford to pay myself! There were occasional weeks when I had to use personal or borrowed money to make payroll until my delinquent clients paid their invoices. Despite the cashflow issues, I still felt the need to be an *Ace of Hearts* employer.

I accomplished this in many ways. I would take one group of employees to breakfast every week. We always sat at the same large round table, requested our usual server, and enjoyed talking and bonding. There may have been some brief company business talk, but most of the conversation was spent getting to know one another. I would also take individual employees to lunch or breakfast for one-on-one relationship building.

A few times a week I bought my office staff lunch. I would personally take all of their food orders and either pick up the meals or have them delivered. I would eat with them and let them share their stories, thoughts, and life with me. Routinely, I'd invite an employee and their family over to my home for dinner. There was always a first-class Christmas party and a summer picnic every year. We would also attend company activities together, such as going to stock car races, demolition derbies, county fairs, and more.

This past weekend I took some of my employees to a hot air balloon festival. I paid for their parking and their entrance fee. They covered their food costs and the cost if they wanted to go for a hot air balloon ride. I saw employees buying each other snacks and drinks, talking and laughing, and enjoying the time they spent together. One of the attendees was Peter, my recent hire from another state. He looked like he was in shock as if he had never experienced working for an *Ace of Hearts* company in his entire life. He was having the time of his life with new his coworkers. He expressed his appreciation many times for my inviting him to the activity, as well as for hiring him. He said with a huge grin, "I want to retire working for your company!"

Off the clock, company activities should always come with a high invitation but a low challenge, meaning to excitingly ask your employees to attend the event without any pressure. Make sure each employee is personally invited and knows the times, dates, location, and other important details about the event. Let them know attendance isn't mandatory and if they are too busy to come, you won't be offended. If it is a family appropriate venue, then invite them to bring their families.

You're Hiring!

Make sure your hiring process facilitates hiring the right people. The process shouldn't be completed hastily and never just to employ a warm body because you need to fill a position. If the hiring process is conducted in such a manner, your applicants and new hires will sense it. They'll immediately know they aren't going to feel valued if they take the job. No one wants to feel like they were hired as a seat warmer in a cubicle to be viewed as employee number 3622, rather than a human being. Feeling that way will result in poor work performance and productivity.

The methods you employ need to help you find employees who have not only talent but also the personal characteristics that will meld with your *Ace of Hearts* organization. You want to hire potential *Ace of Hearts* employees, ones you can develop to fit your company's values and mission. An applicant who lights up the sky like a Fourth of July fireworks finale in the area of skills might look perfect to you until you realize that this same applicant's social skills are a sparkler about to fizzle. NFL coaches aren't recruiting all-star receivers who don't mesh perfectly with the team's quarterback. The football player who possesses the greatest skills but has negative attitudes and actions that distract the team from winning games is worthless. The same thought should apply to your talent search!

CONFUSION ON PROHIBITED QUESTIONS AND ANSWERS

I am shocked at the number of times I've heard HR personnel state the laws which prevent past employers from divulging detrimental information about someone who used to work for them. I've heard an equal number of comments stating there are laws governing what a potential employer can ask. Understand: policy and law are not the same. Policies are internal rules generated by companies, whereas laws are passed by the federal or state government.

I am against company polices that don't allow an employer to comment in detail on someone who previously worked for them. I don't personally make those reference calls anymore, but when I did, I always felt frustrated. Every time I'd speak to someone who could only share employment dates and other general information allowed by law, I always felt I did not get enough information on my potential new hire. The lack of information leads to hiring blunders, which circulates problem employees from company to company. How does that help anyone? Such company policies cost employers a great deal of money. I am not sure how much, but my guess would be millions or even billions of dollars!

THE GIVENS

Everyone puts all of the right stuff on resumes and job applications. At the interview, they also say all the correct buzz words that will get them hired. Anyone applying for a job will always list references who will enthusiastically praise them. No one's listing the name and phone number of a former coworker who despised them. Applicants generally won't share issues they had with past employers or coworkers. They aren't going to tell you they had an attendance or tardiness problem. You are only going to receive information to convince you they are the best person for the position. No cons, only pros! Interviewees will tell you what they think you want to hear. They'll make all sorts of promises, some with intentions of keeping them and some they know they will never keep.

TREAT APPLICANTS AS YOU WANT TO BE TREATED

An application process is already a stressful event for someone to go through. Make sure to treat each candidate extremely well. Do it because it is the right thing to do, but also because it is a reflection of your company. You want people to hear, "I didn't get the job, but every person I dealt with through the process was wonderful!" They might not have been a good fit for the position they applied for, but they might be the perfect fit for a job opening in the future. They should feel so good about the experience that they'd be willing to go through the trouble to apply again, maybe even anticipating another chance, intently watching and waiting for your next job posting.

COVER LETTERS

Cover letters are much more important than resumes.

Unlike a resume, which states facts, lists dates, and is littered with canned phrases and bullet points, a cover letter is more personal. It's a window into the applicant's soul, which allows you to hear what they have to say about themselves. Although it consists of written words, the applicant's "voice" can almost be heard revealing who they truly are. If their cover letter piques your interest and you feel a desire to get to know them better, then move the applicant forward in the application process. My company hiring policies exclude applicants immediately who couldn't be bothered to write a cover letter.

RESUMES

More than the info provided, look for spelling errors, grammar issues, incomplete information, and other unprofessional resume presentation. Did they rush through its composition? Was it neatly formatted and organized? If their resume was carelessly prepared, chances are they will be equally careless performing their job duties. If their resume was compiled in a way that displayed professionalism, then move the applicant to the next step.

SNOOP THE WEB

Google the candidate's name and see what comes up. My company conducts a public records check on individuals we are considering hiring. We can check on driving violations, lawsuits, or criminal charges that have been filed against the applicant. I know I teach accepting employees right where they are and loving them unconditionally; this thinking starts after the hiring process when they become your current employees. To avoid future headaches, it is best to hire people with fewer issues, instead of more, or at least to be aware of potential challenges ahead of time.

Finding a few negatives does not always eliminate an applicant. It may require an adequate response about an issue or issues. You might determine that an applicant who appeared to be careless with his bills, with many lawsuits listed, was inundated with numerous hospital bills because their spouse had been injured in an accident or that someone who committed a crime in their late teens or early adult life has since turned their life around.

SOCIAL MEDIA

Google the names of your candidates and search for them on social media sites such as Facebook, Instagram, Twitter, and others. The comments and photos applicants publicly share could reveal a lot of information about them. You may learn some negatives about an applicant or hopefully some positives or a mix of both. You might find out on a news website that they were a good Samaritan who saved a person choking on food. On the other hand, there may be comments or photos they posted that are distasteful.

Don't allow what you find to be the sole deciding factor on whether to hire someone or not. Make sure you weigh everything from the cover letter, to the resume, to the background check during this stage of the process. If you see a picture or comment that is offensive or would not reflect your company's values, check when they posted it. Was it several years ago? Over time, people can change and evolve into someone very different. It can take several years, or even less time, to change. I have sometimes changed my thoughts and views in a brief amount of time. Recently, something I had thought to be true for most of my life was changed within a matter of days due to an intensive experience I had.

THE INTERVIEW

Start the interview off right with a warm greeting. Introduce yourself and shake the applicant's hand; make the applicant feel comfortable by engaging in casual talk. Transparently tell them a little about yourself both personally and professionally. Share with them how you got hired, what you've experienced since then, and give them information about the company. Describe your role, the role the candidate applied for, and what the company is looking for in an applicant. Look for personality traits that would fit well with the company. Ask questions that are likely to invoke responses that will reveal personal attributes and behavioral characteristics about the applicant. Open-ended questions will force the candidate to talk more in depth. Don't interrupt! Let the applicant talk, and when they slow down or stop, try to encourage them to continue talking.

THE TRUTH WILL SET THEM FREE!!

Encourage applicants to be honest with their answers. Let them know they are applying to work for a company that values transparency and truthfulness. Assure them that knowing their negatives isn't truly negative but provides a way to know the areas where they need mentoring and the spots where a concentrated focus would help them become better: better for them personally and better for the company.

THE LEAST IMPORTANT

When I hire someone, skills, knowledge, and diplomas attained are never my focus. Even less important to me is prior work experience in the same industry, where they claim to know already "how it's done." Some would say such experience is a plus, but it's a complete turn off for me. I have had greater success with raw recruits. They come without bad habits and are easy to train. They make no statements like, "That's not how we did it at ABC company," and they don't push back when you teach them how you want it done. You can easily mold an inexperienced person's skills, thought process, and attitude when they haven't been poisoned by negativity or learning to cut corners.

THE MOST IMPORTANT

The most important thing you need to learn is how to find out who the applicant really is—not what they can do or promise to do, but who they honestly are. Answers to questions like:

- Are they leadable?
- Will they accept mentoring?
- Will mentoring be an effective management style for them?
- Are professional and personal growth important to them?
- Are they a self-starter?
- What is their outlook on life?
- Are they a positive or a negative person?
- What are their personal goals?
- What are their professional goals?

- What job role resonates with them?
- What job role isn't a good fit?
- What personal hobbies and activities do they enjoy?
- Which work tasks inspire and excite them?
- Are they a pronounced communicator?
- Will they be a good team member?
- Are they friendly?
- Do they have acceptable social skills?
- Are they approachable?
- Are they confident but not arrogant?
- Is their body language consistent with a person who is being open or closed?
- Do they seem engaged with you or disengaged?
- What personal and professional baggage do they carry?
- Are they cynical or jaded from past workplace experiences?
- How do they deal with hurts, adversity, and life's challenges?
- Do you see them as an employee with longevity potential?
- Does the salary you are offering cover their life needs? (Notice I did not say wants. I may want a bass boat and a helicopter, but that's not a need!)
- Can you see them easily grafting into your company's *Ace of Hearts* culture?

Analyze what you determined from their answers to the above questions. If it is a negative, can it change? Do the positives outweigh the negatives, even if some of the negatives will never change?

Follow Your Inner Voice

We all have an inner voice that can pick up on the good, bad, and ugly of people and situations. Some people have an inner voice that is more attuned than others; this is something that can be honed and developed with time and experience. You often hear people saying they wish they would have followed their gut! Once you conclude the interview, take some time, 24 to 48 hours, to review how it went. Repeatedly look over notes and mentally review the interview. If you have a hunch, positive or negative about the applicant, you should follow it. The applicant you chose must fit the role they are interviewing for, but more importantly, they must fit into your *Ace of Hearts* culture.

ACE OF HEARTS
ONBOARDING

GREAT NEWS! YOU have now recruited the best candidate possible during the hiring process. Onboarding that candidate is not just the process of integrating a new employee into your organization; it's the second phase of micro-training for your new hire. The opinions new hires form during their onboarding experience will be added to those formed during the hiring process. Proceed with caution! Don't let the process poison them with any negative experiences. To achieve a positive experience, a proper *Ace of Hearts* onboarding process is a must. It should be a confirmation of the positive experiences they received from the "application-to-hired" timeline.

REDUCE ANXIETY

Starting a new job always generates anxiety. The new employee is faced with the daunting task of learning a new job as well as the company culture. There's also the stress created by meeting new people and being in an environment full of unknowns. Your onboarding process should be designed to mitigate those stressors. This process should help advance the *Ace of Hearts* culture you're trying to accomplish.

Employees who experience a proper onboarding process are more likely to remain at a company long term. Money and time spent on hiring and training are greatly reduced when employee turnover rates are kept low. Onboarding, done improperly, will have new employees transitioning into their role with additional feelings of stress and anxiousness. This will handicap their performance and productivity and can lead to an increase in employee turnover.

BE WELCOMING

An *Ace of Hearts* onboarding process will have new employees feeling warmly welcomed to the organization. The onboarding process should feel like a heartfelt invitation for them to join their new workplace family. Don't speed walk them through a company facility tour with all of your employees staring at them as if they're the "new kid at school." Don't overload them with a stack of papers to sign and date, giving them writer's cramp on their first day. Please don't seat them in a small room the size of a broom closet or throw a company policy manual at them and leave them alone to read it. I've seen it happen!

> I was visiting a company when a young man arrived for his first day on the job. He was immediately given the company's standard operating and procedure manual, which was so large that they should have issued him a wheelbarrow for safe transport. They ushered him down a hallway and put him in a tiny

room with no windows. As the door slowly closed, he was told to read the entire manual and sign the acknowledgment page at the end. The door closed, and he was not seen for the first half of the day.

I kept thinking about him all morning. I inquired about him to the person I was meeting. He abruptly brushed me off, "Don't worry about him. He'll be fine." I was worried about him. I was concerned about how much he was negatively being affected by what he was experiencing on his first day. He was in solitary confinement, forced to read a book less exciting than a new refrigerator user guide! I pictured him curled up in a ball muttering to himself when they finally went to check on him.

THE WELCOME PACKET

If time allows, two weeks before the employee's first day, send or give them a packet welcoming them to the company. Not some "boiler plate" welcome letter every new employee receives, but a personalized one. I recommend a handwritten welcome card in an envelope. The welcome packet should further provide instructions pertaining to their first day, the upcoming onboarding process, and other relevant information. All paperwork requiring their signature should also be included. It'll allow them to complete all necessary paperwork and be ready for collection on their first day. Give them a company directory and a map of your company's facilities if it is a large campus.

The packet should also include pertinent information about your company. Provide them with details about the role they were hired to fill and the duties to be performed in their role. Inform them of the company's overall expectations. The details of the expectations should be comprehensive but sensibly and realistically explained. Include a schedule of the upcoming onboarding process and training. Educate the new hire on the company's history, vision, mission, and values. Lastly, introduce them to the company's founders, supervisors, and executives and assign them a mentor. Have recent photos and company bios of these people.

Providing your new hires with a suitable welcome package is a first step to removing the anxiety they are already experiencing about starting a new job—before they start! It will also eliminate the time normally spent reading and signing papers. This will allow you to have the time to entirely focus on your new employee, making sure their first day is a positive experience. Hopefully more than positive! You should strive to have a day so enjoyable they'll wake up excited to come back for day two.

When I hire someone, I want their first day to be like a party celebrating a family member who is returning home after a decade's long journey. I personally wait in the reception area to shake their hand and welcome them to the family. Their direct supervisor and I take them out for an *Ace of Hearts* breakfast at a local restaurant. There's absolutely no business talk discussed during the meal. We spend the whole time

getting to know our new employee. We ask a lot of open-ended questions and do a lot of listening. The goal is for us to talk less, allowing them to talk a whole lot more. For my new employees to feel completely comfortable having a conversation with me and the company management team is so important. This breakfast is the beginning of our relationship, with the overall message being, "Welcome to our company. Never be afraid to communicate with us."

PLAN THE DAY

Onboarding processes are often neglected by companies, causing new employees to feel confused and that their new company is disorganized and poorly run. The lack of such a process can leave new hires feeling unimportant and under-valued. It can cause them to rethink their decision to accept a job with your organization. They might decide that their tenure with you is going to be short-lived.

Your employees' first day shouldn't be an event you extemporize. If you want it to be memorable for them, you'll need to prepare for it in advance. You'll want to have a written schedule organizing the day. Organize it to accomplish the day's goals, but also keep it flexible with extra time between scheduled items. Neither you nor your new hire should ever feel rushed. You don't want to make them feel they are on a factory conveyor belt!

PREPARE YOUR TEAM

Make sure everyone on your staff is aware that it's a new hire's first day. Reinforce the importance of everyone's being friendly, personable, and welcoming. Remind them of the anxiety they went through on their first day. Ask them to imagine what the day would have been like if they had been treated poorly. Would they have looked forward to returning the next day if they had been left feeling unaccepted and unwelcomed? Encourage them to make it their mission for the day to do something to reduce the new person's stress.

PREPARE A SPECIAL PLACE

Your employee's workplace or desk should be carefully prepared for them and ready to use. Have their computer or other equipment set up beforehand so it doesn't delay the plans for the day. Present them with their company identification, parking pass, keys, card swipe, or anything else every employee is given.

My company was contracted to assess employee satisfaction at a large company. If I named the company, most readers would recognize it. You'd think that a giant, worldwide company would have an onboarding process, but they did not. They desperately needed one! The way they orientated their new hires was disorganized and ineffective. Not one employee conveyed their happiness with either the hiring process or their initiation into the company.

One employee commented that on his first day he was promised a set of keys, a personal locker, and some job-specific tools he needed. A few weeks went by, and none of those promises had been fulfilled. He decided to remind his supervisor, but when he did, he wished he hadn't bothered. The gruff reply he got, combined with a few explicit words, was, "I don't want to ******* hear it. You're just the ******* new guy. We'll get around to it when we get around to it. Now get your *** back to work!"

Another employee asked for help on using a piece of equipment. The equipment wasn't just a harmless copy machine or a postage stamp machine. This was the type of equipment that could have injured or even killed someone. He said his supervisor acted bothered and barked, "I don't know how to run it. Ask Robby; he'll get you dialed in." When he asked Robby, he exploded in anger, aggressively yelling, "I'm not paid to teach you a thing! I'm not paid extra to be a trainer, and if I was, I wouldn't want to train you!" The employee gave up seeking help. He taught himself how to run the equipment and ended up personally buying the tools he had been promised. A few months later he was given his keys, and a year later he was finally assigned a locker.

Consider taking your new employees out for breakfast when they arrive. Introduce them to their coworkers and managers with more than just a hello, a handshake, and a nod. Let them have some time to initiate the bonding process with the people they meet.

Assign someone you carefully selected to mentor your new hire. Assigning a mentor is one of the most important things you can do for a new employee. A mentor should facilitate an employee's smooth transition into their new role.

Choosing the right mentor will often be the biggest factor in motivating effectively and determining how productive your new employee will be. Don't randomly choose and assign just anyone to fill the role of mentor. Mentors should be employees completely committed to your company's vision, mission, and values. Only choose individuals for this important role who are a picture of what an *Ace of Hearts* mentor should be.

Remeet, Regreet, and Eat

During day one, reinforce important details your new hires received in their welcome packet. This shouldn't be done all at once, but in short "snack bite" conversations throughout the day at different intervals. Talk about and encourage them to ask questions about your expectations. Constantly engage them in conversation and urge them to ask you questions about anything. Take them on a tour of the company facilities and describe what work is performed in the various departments. Inform them of the resources available to them and give them a schedule of the upcoming training planned for them.

Give thought to scheduling an end-of-day bread-breaking time, which will serve as a remeet and regreet with their new coworkers. It will allow the new employees to reconnect with the coworkers they met earlier in the day and help pair people's names to their faces.

If you decide to have this activity, cater in some hors d'oeuvres and beverages. The event should be scheduled to begin an hour or two before the shift finishes for the day. Of course, business still must be conducted, but this can be accomplished by having a skeleton crew handle business operations while others attend the event. To ensure everyone gets time to interact, rotate your staff in and out of the event.

TRAINING

Your training needs to be determined and designed to clearly fit your company's objectives. It should cover skills, abilities, knowledge, employee development, and other corporate specific topics. Include training that fosters your company's culture goals, builds on the personal mentoring your employees receive, and provides individual training. Consider offering life courses to your employees. Enhancing their life outside of the workplace enhances their life inside the workplace. It makes them happier people, better citizens, and better employees!

Your training should be professionally developed. It shouldn't be lengthy or boring, but a combination of live training, online courses, and one-on-one interaction with a mentor. All testing, grades, and certificates should be organized and stored online.

ASSESSMENT

Routinely check in with your new employees during the onboarding process. Solicit honest and transparent feedback. Assure them that the information they share is greatly appreciated and invaluable to your company. Their feedback will help you ensure the process you have in place is effective. The data you gather can help you determine if you need to add, remove, tweak, or totally rework how you onboard people.

Conclusion

Getting my Voice Back

I have been an entrepreneur and business owner since shortly after graduating from high school. My first few businesses were part-time, one-man operations. In those days my full-time job required 50 to 60 hours a week to pay my bills, so I ran my business during my off hours. I was disappointed in the way most business owners operated their businesses and how poorly they treated their employees. Those experiences caused me to promise myself that when I owned a business that had employees, I was going to do things completely different.

When the time came, I kept my promise. From the beginning, I was always an *Ace of Hearts* leader and business owner but was unaware of that fact. Over the years I've operated my companies and followed the concepts I've shared in this book, but I had never associated what I was doing with the phrase *Ace of Hearts*.

I have been blessed with an amazing wife and children. I've enjoyed a life far better than I could have ever asked for, but I'm no different from anyone else on the planet. I've experienced more than my fair share of failures, hurts, abandonments, and betrayals. Through those letdowns, I never stopped believing there was any better way to act professionally and personally than the *Ace of Hearts* way.

Those years of repeated adversity began to take a heavy toll on me spiritually, mentally, emotionally, and physically. I felt drained by all of the years of investing in others and not feeling anyone was investing in me. Burnout began to set in, so I decided to take time away from the business world. I traveled and lived abroad for over seven years.

I barricaded myself behind emotional walls of protection, limited my relationships to a few close friends, and wasn't interested in building new ones. I didn't realize it, but I had become one of those hurting people I used to accept and love unconditionally. I wasn't loving others like I used to, and no one was showing me any love. My *Ace of Hearts* lifestyle slowly faded and became a faint memory.

I hoped taking a long break would rejuvenate and energize me. It did not! I began asking my wife, "Is the old Brad gone forever? Will I ever make it back to where I used to be? Is this the beginning of the end?"

Almost by accident, I founded an online startup company that landed me back in the Chicagoland area. The company was successful, ran on auto pilot, and didn't require a lot of attention. I found myself relieved that I didn't have a need for employees. I rested easy, knowing there would be no pressure to love and invest in anyone but my family and myself.

One morning I received an email from a friend of mine who lives in Chiang Mai, Thailand.

Brad,

I want to introduce you to Michael Woolstrum. I met him back in August when he was here on business. He was a keynote speaker at a men's conference in Bangkok. I am going to send out an introduction email to both of you. I think the two of you would get along great, and networking together could be very beneficial to both of you. He is also the CEO of Touch International, a company which has contracts with various U.S. government, military, aviation, and agriculture

industries. He is also a pastor of a church in Texas and oversees a nonprofit organization.
Jeff

I reluctantly responded to the introduction and emailed Michael. I wasn't sure where this original communication was going to end up, but I decided that if I ended up going into business with this man I had been introduced to, that was as far as I was going to allow the relationship to go. I was determined to keep Michael Woolstrum safely located outside of the battle-ready emotional walls I had erected. I wasn't going to allow myself to be hurt again.

Michael and I shared two phone calls. The first was while he was standing in line about to board an airplane. We quickly shared what we both were doing in business and some of the companies we had previously owned. As we hung up, Michael said, "Call me soon." The call was short and sweet, and no personal questions were asked. I was relieved!

Over the next three weeks, we shared a couple of brief emails that followed up on what we had talked about. Those three weeks were extremely busy for me. I had a break in my schedule, so I decided to call him. A few minutes into the conversation, Michael said, "Brad, I don't want to do business with you."

I was stunned. Thank goodness I didn't get to know him more. This certainly would have turned out badly.

Michael then continued, "That's not what I do. I don't just do business with people. I don't just employ people. I 'do life' with them."

I thought, Where in the world is this going?

He then bluntly stated, "Brad, you've been stung many times over, in business, by friends, by family, and in church. You're about to get unstung. I've got to go. Don't ever wait three weeks to call me again." No other words were said, except we both said bye. The call ended, and I found myself staring at the screen of my mobile phone for what seemed like an eternity.

My mind began to race. What was he talking about? How did he know I have been hurt—or stung as he put it?" I then got a little angry with Jeff, my friend who had introduced us. He must have told him I had been hurt in the past. They must be trying to hatch some plan to "fix" me. I don't need anyone to fix me! I am doing just fine by myself. As I thought of those last two words—by myself—I immediately experienced a great feeling of loneliness and hopelessness.

I spent the rest of the day and evening trying to forget about Michael and our conversation. It didn't work. In fact, it completely consumed my thoughts. I attempted to concentrate on my work, but what had been said on the phone distracted me.

As I was driving home, I tried to analyze the nonsense I had heard earlier. I "do life" with people? Come on! I've got people I "do life" with too—my wife and family. I don't have time to "do life" with anyone but them. He doesn't know me, and I don't know him. How can you "do life" with a stranger? I wondered if there was something wrong with him.

I got home and took my Labrador, Boomer, outside to play ball. I threw the ball, and he ran after it. Suddenly I replayed in my head another sentence this Michael guy had said: "Don't ever wait three weeks to call me again." No CEO wants to be bothered with a bunch of phone calls, especially ones not related to business. And didn't he say, "Brad, I don't want to do business with you?" If he doesn't want to do business with me, how does talking to me do anything for him? What's in it for him? I looked down and found Boomer patiently waiting with his ball in his mouth.

I went inside and tried to relax until dinner. It didn't happen. I continued to think about Michael's words. My wife started making dinner, so I walked to the bathroom to wash up. As I was washing my hands, I remembered his saying, "You're about to get unstung." I said aloud, "Really, Michael Woolstrum? Who do you think you are? I don't need your help." I looked in the mirror at myself and saw a man I did not recognize. I looked weary and old, and my eyes had lost their once hopeful gleam. I knew I needed to make a change, but was "getting unstung" with the help of Michael Woolstrum the answer?

That evening I ate dinner in silence. My wife looked at me with a smile and asked me what was wrong. I reluctantly told her about my recent interactions with Michael Woolstrum. She asked, "What's the problem? It sounds like getting to meet this man is exactly what you need."

I shared my apprehensions with her, "I don't mind doing business with him, but what if it develops into something more? More personal?"

"So, what if it does?" she asked.

"I don't want to get involved in a relationship I think is good, only to find out it's bad, that it was a farce."

"You won't know unless you try," she replied. "Some relationships go bad, some don't last, and others are just so-so.

But there are going to be two or three or even more that are awesome. Maybe even life-changing!"

"Great, that means I must sift through a whole lot of bad, hoping for the ones which are worthwhile," I complained.

She expounded, "I remember the Brad Shrader who thought anyone was worth investing in. You always took the time to get to know everybody. You loved people without expectations or anything in return. You told me, no matter what the outcome was going to be, it was always worth it. Maybe not always for you, but for the other person." Then she added, "You may have had some hurts and disappointments along the way but loving others and allowing others to love you will outweigh any negatives you experience on the journey."

I decided to ignore her. The dinner table was quiet for several minutes, so she broke the silence again. "This man Michael sounds a lot like the husband I used to know. I could be wrong, but I have the feeling he's exactly what you have needed in your life for several years. Maybe he isn't, but we will never know unless you give him a chance. It's not fair that you are making decisions about him based on your past hurts. They are your hurts, not his."

"Hey, that's life. Lots of people haven't given me a chance when I deserved it!" I snapped.

"Honey, I know two who did," she calmly replied. "Me and Jesus. What if the two of us decided you weren't worth it?"

The next morning and for many months, Michael Woolstrum and I communicated often by phone, email, and in person. We developed a wonderful relationship of love, trust, and acceptance—both personally and professionally. We began to do business together. We began to do personal activities together. We began to do ministry together. We began to "do life" together!

He shared his relationship philosophy with me, and I began to follow it.

- Do what you say you will do – integrity.
- Communicate clearly and often – efficient
- Finish what you start – effective
- Work on body, soul & spirit – holistic

He insisted I be transparent with him about everything. I voiced my concerns, feeling if he didn't like what he heard, things might go badly between us. He firmly replied, "I love you. I'll never cast you aside." Even with that assurance, I often feared that one day he'd probably be done with me, that he would stop taking my calls or answering my emails. Not only did that not happen, but our communication increased even more.

One weekend we had a seminar in my area. I had always doubted my influence with the acquaintances, friends, and employees I had interacted with over the years. I felt that no matter how hard I tried; I had not made a difference in the lives of the people I knew. Almost thirty people with whom I had some sort of relationship attended the two-day seminar. Michael asked each person to introduce themselves, share something about themselves, and tell how they knew me.

What I heard during the meet-and-greet session for the seminar humbled me like never before. Every person expressed their love for me and their gratitude for something I had done that had bettered their life. Many claimed I had offered them a helping hand when no one else would, at a time in their life when they needed it the most. Others said that something I had said or done had changed their behavior or their life in a positive way that could not be quantified.

I did not remember most of the stories I heard. I certainly did not realize the positive impact my actions had. The seminar confirmed what my wife had said months earlier: regardless of the outcome that results from investing in people, it is always worth it.

As an *Ace of Hearts* leader, the relationships that don't turn out as you expected often come with some really bad hurts. You'll frequently find yourself disappointed and frustrated. There will be days you'll feel completely exhausted and that you have nothing else to give. Despite all of those negatives, I promise that the *Ace of Hearts* journey of "doing life" with people is more than worth it. The satisfaction you'll experience when you see the lives of those you're investing in being transformed is worth more than any fortune you might amass.

Don't give up on trying to be an *Ace of Hearts* person to someone and don't stop an *Ace of Hearts* person from investing in you. You won't know if the next person you meet is going to be the Brad Shrader who desperately needs your love or the Michael Woolstrum by whom you need to be loved. Or you might just be some shy, lonely seventh grader's Edmund Crabb. The next man or woman you meet might even become your *Ace of Hearts* spouse!

Training Lion Services

We offer over 100 quality online employee courses FREE of Charge with our *Ace of Hearts* Leadership course package. All testing, grades, and certificates are organized and stored online. If you are interested in the development of first-class, professional training material, Training Lion offers this as one of their many services. We can also host your proprietary company training on our Learning Management System (LMS). If you would like us to develop a custom-built LMS for your company, our team of designers and programmers can professionally build one for you. Please visit our website www.traininglion.com or contact us at adaniels@traininglion.com.

Notes

www.ingramcontent.com/pod-product-compliance
Lightning Source LLC
Chambersburg PA
CBHW071551200326
41519CB00021BB/6704